Oxford International English

5

Izabella Hearn
Myra Murby
Moira Brown

OXFORD
UNIVERSITY PRESS

OXFORD
UNIVERSITY PRESS

Great Clarendon Street, Oxford OX2 6DP

Oxford University Press is a department of the University of Oxford.
It furthers the University's objective of excellence in research, scholarship,
and education by publishing worldwide in

Oxford New York

Auckland Cape Town Dar es Salaam Hong Kong Karachi
Kuala Lumpur Madrid Melbourne Mexico City Nairobi
New Delhi Shanghai Taipei Toronto

With offices in

Argentina Austria Brazil Chile Czech Republic France Greece
Guatemala Hungary Italy Japan Poland Portugal Singapore
South Korea Switzerland Thailand Turkey Ukraine Vietnam

© Oxford University Press 2013

The moral rights of the authors have been asserted

Database right Oxford University Press (maker)

First published 2013

British Library Cataloguing in Publication Data

Data available

ISBN- 978-019-838881-4

20 19 18 17 16

Printed in India by Multivista Global Pvt.Ltd.

Paper used in the production of this book is a natural, recyclable product made from wood
grown in sustainable forests. The manufacturing process conforms to the environmental
regulations of the country of origin.

Acknowledgements
The publisher and authors would like to thank the following for permission to use photographs
and copyright material:

p9t: Chin Kit Sen/Shutterstock; p9: Djordje Radivojevic/Shutterstock; p14t: Moria Brown; p14b:
Caro/Alamy; p19: Monkey Business Images/Shutterstock; p22: Carl Warner; p23t: natalystudio/
Shutterstock; p23b: caldix/Shutterstock; p25: ronstik/Shutterstock; p28m: Tristan Tan/
Shutterstock; p28b: MaxPhotographer/Shutterstock; p28t: vso/Shutterstock; p29t: (c) Camilla
M. Mann / With a Lens and a Pen.; p29b: highviews/Shutterstock; p29m: olneystudio/Alamy;
p34t: Dzm1try/Shutterstock; p30: Madlen/Shutterstock; p34: Morton Beebe/Corbis; p34b:
bluestocking/iStockphoto; p34m: Africa Studio/Shutterstock; p35l: Iraidka/Shutterstock; p35m:
martan/Shutterstock; p35r: J. Helgaso/Shutterstock; p36b: nodff/Shutterstock; p37t: Dr. Morley
Read/Shutterstock; p37m: irabel8/Shutterstock; p37b: Alaska Stock/Alamy; p39: Khoroshunova
Olga/Shutterstock; p42m: Stubblefield Photography; p42b: Martin Harvey/Alamy; p43: Martin
Harvey/Alamy; p49r: Mark A. Johnson/Corbis; p49t: Claudio Divizia/Shutterstock; p49l: andrej
pol/Shutterstock; p52t: © Hergé/Moulinsart 2012; p52b: Pageflip publishing; p52: Mitar
Vidakovic/Shutterstock; p53: thephoenixcomic.co.uk; p58: Photos 12/Alamy; p59l: Photos 12/
Alamy; p59r: Photos 12/Alamy; p59t: MovieStoreCollection; p63: © Hergé/Moulinsart 2012;
p66bl: Flip Schulke/Corbis; p66tr: Douglas Miller/Stringer/Hulton Archive/Getty Images; p66tl:
Nyein Chan Naing/epa/Corbis; p66br: Micheline Pelletier/Corbis; p67tr: Bettmann/Corbis; p67tl:
Alison Wright/Corbis; p67bl: Bettmann/Corbis; p67br: Punit Paranjpe/Stringer/Corbis; p69: Mary
Evans Picture Library; p72: David Turnley/Corbis; p77: Rozhkovs/Shutterstock; p78: Winchester
College/In aid of Mary Seacole Memorial Statue Appeal/Mary Evans; p79a: Mary Evans Picture
Library; p79b: Getty Images; p79b: © Corbis; p79d: JeremyRichards / Shutterstock.com; p80b:
Simon Price/Alamy; p80r: Getty Images; p80l: Marco De Swart/AFP/Getty Images; p83: Ernest
C. Withers/© Minnesota Historical Society/Corbis; p86: AFP/Getty Images; p87: ibisailing.co.uk
p91: Getty Images; p96tl: Aping Vision/STS/Getty Images; p96tr: Tom Gilks/Alamy; p96br: MJTH/
Shutterstock; p96bl: Forster Forest/Shutterstock; p97: razihusin/Shutterstock; p97: Avesun/
Shutterstock; p97: Andy Dean Photography/Shutterstock; p97: Patryk Kosmider/Shutterstock;
p97: Daboost/Shutterstock; p102l: firstnews.co.uk; p102r: archana bhartia/shutterstock; p108:
Paul Seward, Farm Input Promotions Africa Ltd.; p109t: Francois van Heerden/Shutterstock;
p109b: Belinda Pretorius/Shutterstock; p110c: Look at Sciences/Science Photo Library;
p110a: John Foxx/Stockbyte/Getty Images; p110d: Andi Duff /Alamy; p110b: Evolution1088/
Dreamstime; p111: © Corbis; p116: Melvyn Longhurst/Alamy; p117: JTB MEDIA CREATION, Inc./
Alamy; p125: Getty Images; p124: Removing the Thorn (St. Jerome or Androcles and the Lion),
2007 (acrylic on canvas & painted wood frame)/Bridgman Art Library; p130: Hanley Museum &
Art Gallery, Staffordshire, UK / The Bridgeman Art Library; p131: Jorgen Udvang/iStockphoto.
com; p138tr: National Geographic; p138tl: Rex Features; p139l: AFP/Getty Images; p139r:
Corbis; p144: Getty Images; p154: Virgin Galactic; p146: Alonzo Design/i-Stockphoto; p147:
Amenhotepov/Shutterstock; p148t: guentermanaus/Shutterstock; p148b: Ocean/Corbis; p149:
Jami Tarris/Workbook Stock/Getty; p151b: kated/Shutterstock; p151t: OUP/Photodisc.

Background Images: Devation/Edwin Verbruggen/Shutterstock; Vector/Shutterstock; Telnov
Oleksii/Shutterstock; Denis Tabler/Shutterstock; nodff/Shutterstock; Dmitry Smirnov/
Dreamstime; Aleksandr Bryliaev/Shutterstock; Konyaeva/Shutterstock; Oculo/Shutterstock;
badahos/Shutterstock; kanate/Shutterstock.

Cover illustration: Hollie Hibbert

Artwork is by: Laura Anderson; Mark Beech; Stefan Chabluk; Katriona Chapman; Chris Coady;
Russ Daff; Niall Harding; Michael Heath; Hollie Hibbert; Carol Liddiment; Lizzie Lissimore;
Francisca Marquez; Melanie Matthews; Chiara Pasqualotto; Dusan Pavlic; Kate Rochester; Emma
Shaw Smith; Meilo So; Mike Spoor; Katri Valkamo; Bee Willey.

The author and publisher are grateful for permission to reprint the following copyright
material:

Lillian Allan: 'Anancy' from *If You See the Truth: Poems for Children and Young People* (Verse to
Vinyl, 1990), copyright © Lillian Allen 1987, used by permission of the author

Dominic Barker: extract from *The Big Story* (Project X, OUP, 2009), reprinted by permission of
Oxford University Press.

Andy Blackford: 'Tchang and the Pearl Dragon' from *Myths and Legends: Dragon Tales* (ORT
Treetops, OUP, 2010), copyright © Andy Blackford 2010, reprinted by permission of Oxford
University Press.

Betsy Byars: extract from *The Cartoonist* (Viking/Bodley Head, 1978), copyright © Betsy Byars
1978, reprinted by permission of the author.

Jane Clarke: 'Finding a Friend', copyright © Jane Clarke 1999, first published in *I Wanna be Your
Mate* compiled by Tony Bradman (Bloomsbury, 1999), reprinted by permission of the author.

Afua Cooper: lines from 'Kensington Market', from *The Red Caterpillar on College Street*, (Sister
Vision Press, 1989), reprinted by permission of the author

Roald Dahl: extract from *Charlie and the Chocolate Factory* (Puffin, 2007), reprinted by permission
of David Higham Associates.

Bob Dylan: 'Blowin' in the Wind', lyrics by Bob Dylan, copyright © 1962, © renewed 1990 by
Special Rider Music, administered by Sony/ATV Music Publishing and reprinted with their
permission. All rights reserved.

Cherie Emigh: 'Home Country. What's That?' by Hunter Emigh from *Slurping Soup and other
confusions: true stories and activities to help third culture kids during transition* by Maryan Afnan
Ahmad, Cherie Emigh, Ulrike Gemmer, Barbara Menezes, Kathryn Tonges and Lucinda
Willshire, www.slurpingsoup.com 2010, copyright © 2010 Slurping Soup and Other Confusions,
reprinted by permission of the co-authors.

Richard Erdoes and Alfonzo Ortiz (Eds.):'Grandmother Spider Steals the Sun' a tale
reported by James Mooney in the 1890s from *American Indian Myths and Legends* (Pantheon Books,
1984), copyright © 1984 by Richard Erdoes and Alfonzo Ortiz, reprinted by permission of
pantheon Books, a division of Random House, Inc.

John Fardell: extract from *The Flight of the Silver Turtle* (Faber, 2006), copyright © John Fardell
2006, reprinted by permission of the publishers, Faber and Faber Ltd and G P Putnams Sons, a
division of Penguin Group (USA) Inc.

First News: web page adapted from 'team' and 'subscribe' pages at www.firstnews co.uk, by
permission of First News.

Crystal Hubbard: extract from *Catching the Moon: The Story of a Young Girl's Baseball Dream*
illustrated by Randy DuBurke (Lee & Low, 2005), text copyright © 2005 by Crystal Hubbard,
reprinted by permission of Lee and Low books, Inc, New York, NY 10016.

Eva Ibbotson: extract from *Journey to the River Sea* (Macmillan, 2011), reprinted by permission
of Macmillan Children's Books, London, UK.

Mike Jubb: 'Hate Becomes Love', copyright © Mike Jubb 2012, from www.teachkidspoetry.co.
uk, reprinted by permission of the author.

Martin Kiszko: 'Blue Planet's Blue' from *Green Poems for a Blue Planet* (Wild Idea Ltd, 2012),
copyright © Martin Kiszko 2010, reprinted by permission of Sheil Land Associates Ltd for the
author.

Kathleen V Kudlinski: extract from *Gandhi, Young Nation Builder* (Childhood of World Figures,
Aladdin, 2006), text copyright © Kathleen Kudlinski 2006, reprinted by permission of Aladdin
Paperbacks, an imprint of Simon & Schuster Children's Publishing Division.

Michael Morpurgo: extract from *Kensuke's Kingdom* (Egmont, 1999), reprinted by permission of
David Higham Associates.

Brian Moses: 'Running the Marathon' from *Olympic Poems* by Brian Moses and Roger Stevens
(Macmillan, 2012), and 'Dreamer' from *Hippopotamus Dancing and Other Poems* (Cambridge
University Press, 1994), reprinted by permission of the author.

Michael Rosen: 'Words Are Ours' from *Michael Rosen's Big Book of Bad Things* (Puffin, 2010),
copyright Michael Rosen 2010, reprinted by permission of Penguin Books Ltd and United
Agents (www.unitedagents.co.uk) on behalf of Michael Rosen.

Ermine Saner: extract from 'Laura Dekker: a heroine for our times', *The Guardian*, 24.1.2012,
copyright © Guardian News & Media Ltd 2012, reprinted by permission of GNM.

Shel Silverstein: 'There's a Light in the Attic' from *A Light in the Attic* (HarperCollins, 1981),
copyright © Shel Silverstein 1974, copyright © 1981, renewed 2002 by Evil Eye Music, LLC; and
'New World' from *Falling Up* (HarperCollins, 1996), copyright © Shel Silverstein 1974, copyright
© 1996, renewed 2002 by Evil Eye Music, LLC, reprinted by permission of David Grossman
Literary Agency Ltd, and HarperCollins Publishers, USA.

Any third party use of this material, outside of this publication, is prohibited. Interested
parties should apply to the copyright holders indicated in each case.

Although we have made every effort to trace and contact all copyright holders before
publication this has not been possible in all cases. If notified, the publisher will rectify any
errors or omissions at the earliest opportunity.

Contents

A world of stories, poems and facts

ARCTIC OCEAN

EUROPE

ASIA

ND

ANY

IRAN

CHINA

JAPAN

EGYPT

U.A.E

INDIA

MYANMAR

A

AFRICA

INDIAN
OCEAN

SOUTH AFRICA

OCEANIA

NEW ZEALAND

UTHERN OCEAN

Unit contents

Unit	Theme	Country focus	Reading and comprehension
1	Who am I?	Brazil, China, Germany, France, USA	**Fiction** Mystery narrative *A New Life for Maia* **Non-fiction** Interview *Home country, what's that?* **Poem** *Finding a Friend*
2	Food, feasts and festivals	Mexico , Canada, Jamaica	**Fiction** Fantasy narrative *The Miracle* **Non-fiction** Historical report *The Origins of Chocolate* **Poem** *Kensington Market*
3	Our blue planet	World's oceans	**Fiction** Adventure narrative *Storm at Sea* **Non-fiction** Food chain reference *Life in the Sea* **Poem** *Dreamer*
			REVISE AND CHECK UNITS 1–3
4	Stories and comic strips	Belgium, UAE	**Fiction** Narrative *The Cartoonist* **Non-fiction** Instruction text *Making an animated film* **Poem** Short verse *Light in the attic, New world*
5	World change makers	India, Iran, USA, South Africa, Myanmar, UK, Jamaica, Russia	**Fiction** Historical life story *The Young Gandhi - All Living Things* **Non-fiction** Biography *Nelson Mandela – Early Years* **Song** Lyrics *Blowin' In The Wind* **Poem** Morphing poem *Hate becomes Love*
6	Sport and health	USA, Holland, New Zealand	**Fiction** Sports star childhood *The Winning Run* **Non-fiction** Blog diary *Sailing Solo* **Poem** List sports poem *The Marathon*
			REVISE AND CHECK UNITS 4–6
7	Making the news	Tanzania, Namibia	**Fiction** Humourous narrative *The Big Story* **Non-fiction** Newspaper article and persuasive advert *First News* **Poem** Humorous list poem *Words Are Ours*
8	Flying high	France, Egypt	**Fiction** Suspense narrative *The Silver Turtle Takes Off* **Non-fiction** Information text *It's all hot air* **Poem** Space adventure *Soft Landings*
9	Tales and legends	Ancient Greece, China, Jamaica, Africa, Canada	**Fiction** A legend from China *Tchang and the Pearl Dragon* **Non-fiction** Instructions *How to make and paint a willow pattern plate* **Poem** *Anancy* **Reading fiction** *Tchang and the Pearl Dragon* (the full story on page 154)
10	Fabulous future	Japan, USA, UK, Nigeria	**Fiction** Science fiction / fantasy *All Summer in a Day* **Non-fiction** Magazine article *The golden ticket to outer space* **Poem** Conservation poem *Blue Planet's Blue*
			REVISE AND CHECK 7–10
			READING FICTION *Tchang and the Pearl Dragon*

Language, grammar, spelling, vocabulary, phonics	Writing	Speaking and listening
• Compound and complex sentences • Spellings of unstressed vowels • Pronouns • Silent vowels	Non-fiction Writing an autobiography	Organization of ideas
• Thesaurus and extension of vocabulary • Direct speech and punctuation • Suffixes and spelling of –y endings • Non-fiction vocabulary • Adverbs • Poetic imagery and language • Specialized non-fiction vocabulary	Non-fiction Writing a factual recount	Language choices
• Unfamiliar words, definitions • Metaphorical expressions and figures of speech • Spelling: words ending in –e and –y, doubling consonants • Commas in complex sentences • Clauses within sentences; connectives	Fiction Writing an adventure story Writing a sea narrative story Non-fiction Note-taking	Group roles and responsibilities
• Unfamiliar words, definitions • Features of fiction genres • Adverbs • Prepositions • Word roots and derivations • Adverbial phrases • Rhyme and alliteration	Fiction Writing a cartoon strip story Writing a screenplay	Confident talking in extended turns Character ideas through drama
• Writer's imagery and techniques • Prepositions • Commas in complex sentences • Spelling and pluralisation • Suffixes and prefixes	Non-fiction Writing a biography Writing a description	Organization of ideas
• New words in context • Direct and reported speech • Dialogue and punctuation • Unfamiliar words, definitions • Commas in complex sentences	Non-fiction Writing a diary	Questions – ideas and understanding Poetry performance
• Unfamiliar words, definitions • Opposites, *example*: un–, im– • Grammatical homophones • Idiomatic phrases • Spelling strategies and suffixes	Non-fiction Writing a narrative news story	Expressing opinions
• Conventions of standard English • Agreement of verbs • Synonyms • Spellings – words ending in –ed, –ing and –y • Rules for doubling consonants • Strategies for spelling and misspelt words	Fiction Writing a suspense story	Questions – develop ideas and extend understanding Organization of ideas
• Pronouns • Commas and complex sentences • Apostrophes – possession and shortened forms • Features of traditional tales and legends	Fiction Writing a traditional tale or legend	Expressing opinions
• Unfamiliar words, definitions, new words in context • Features of fiction genres • Pronouns • Thesaurus and extension of vocabulary • Specialized vocabulary	Non-fiction Writing a formal letter	Poetry performance

1 Who am I?

Let's Talk

1 What do you think the image above is about?
2 Name the different things that you can see in the image.
3 What pictures would you have if it was you in the centre?

"Oh, I get by with a little help from my friends"
John Lennon

What makes you the person you are?

Learning objective
Shape and organize ideas clearly when speaking to aid listener.

A

Create a thought map with all the things, activities and people that are most important to you. Here's an example to give you some ideas.

- My parents and my grandparents
- Drama club
- Eating *goreng pisang* (banana fritters) at festival time
- My cousins in Kuala Lumpur
- My friends Laura, Nellie and Jake
- Playing basketball for my team
- Playing guitar
- My pet cat Fluffy
- Listening to music and buying new clothes

Glossary

culture all the traditions and customs of a group of people

identity who somebody is

nationality the right to belong to a particular country

personality your personality is the type of person you are

Word Cloud

bold · gentle
brave · lively
clever · optimistic
determined · pessimistic
easy-going · shy
funny

B

1 Compare your thought map with a partner. What things are different? What are the same?

2 What other things make up your identity? Look at the list below and decide which three are the most important.

name   family   food   languages spoken

nationality (the country of your passport)

home town or city (where you live now)

hair and eye colour   character or personality

C

Every person is unique. Like your fingerprint, no one else is exactly the same as you.

Plan a short talk to present to the class and include:

- a description of the items in your thought map
- an explanation of why you chose the three most important things that form your identity
- use drawings or images to hold the interest of your listeners.

Journey to the River Sea

 Learning objective
Identify the point of view from which a story is told.

Maia, an orphan living at a boarding school in England, longs for a family and her own home. During class one day, news arrives to say that she must move to another country and start a new life.

Word Cloud

bare	maze
burrowed	rustling
cause	trailing
emigrated	wisdom
laden	

A New Life for Maia

In the room full of fair and light brown heads, she stood out, with her pale triangular face, her widely spaced dark eyes. Her ears, laid bare by the heavy rope of black hair, gave her an unprotected look.

The door opened. Twenty heads turned.

5   "Would Maia Fielding come to the headteacher's room, please?" said the maid.

Maia rose to her feet. *Fear is the cause of all evil*, she told herself, but she was afraid. Afraid of the future… afraid of the unknown. Afraid in the way of someone who is alone in the world.

10   Miss Banks was sitting behind her desk. Mr Murray was in a leather chair by a table, rustling papers. He was Maia's guardian, but he was also a lawyer and never forgot it.

"Well, Maia, we have good news," said Miss Banks. "We have found your relatives…"

15   Maia took a deep breath. *A home*. She had spent her holidays for the past two years in the school. Everyone was friendly and kind but a *home*…

"We have been searching for anyone related to your late father," Mr Murray continued. "We knew that there was a
20 second cousin, a Mr Clifford Carter, that had emigrated six years earlier. He had left England with his family. He is living – the Carters are living – on the Amazon."

"In South America. In Brazil," put in Miss Banks.

Maia lifted her head. "On the *Amazon*?" she said. "In the jungle,
25 do you mean?"

She began thinking of the Amazon. Of rivers full of leeches, of dark forests with hostile Indians with blowpipes, and nameless insects which burrowed into flesh. How could she live there?...

That night Maia sat alone in the library, and she read and she read
30 and she read. She read about the great broad-leaved trees of the rainforest pierced by sudden rays of sun. She read about the travellers who had explored the maze of rivers and found a thousand plants and animals that had never been seen before. She read about brilliantly coloured birds flashing between the laden branches – macaws and
35 humming birds and parakeets – and butterflies the size of saucers and curtains of sweetly scented orchids trailing from the trees. She read about the wisdom of the Indians who could cure sickness and wounds that no one in Europe understood...

Maia looked up from the books. I can do it, she vowed. I will!

From *Journey to the River Sea* by Eva Ibbotson

Glossary

guardian a person who looks after an orphan

hostile very unfriendly and ready to fight

leeches small worms that stick to the skin and suck out blood

vowed made a serious promise to yourself

Comprehension

Use words and phrases from the extract to support your answers.

1 Which two statements about Maia are true?

   a Maia has light brown hair.

   b Maia does not have any parents.

   c Maia lives in Brazil.

   d Maia feels afraid of the future.

What do you think?

1 Why do you think the writer describes Maia's hair as a 'heavy rope'?

2 What phrase in line 15 shows that Maia is trying to be brave?

3 Why does the writer repeat the word 'home' in lines 15 and 17?

4 Find two phrases in the last line that show Maia was curious to learn about the Amazon and willing to try and live there.

C

What about you?

Have you had to move to a new place? What words would describe how you felt before you moved?

Using 'but' correctly

Learning objective
Explore ways of combining simple sentences and re-ordering clauses to make compound and complex sentences.

The conjunction 'but' is often used to indicate a contrast that would not be expected after the first clause. ***Example***: In *Journey to the River Sea,* Maia says: 'Fear is the cause of all evil, she told herself, but she was afraid.'

A

Finish the sentences below by adding a contrast that would not be expected from the first clause.

1   I looked happy, but...

2   Johan was very nervous about his first day at senior school, but...

3   Tchai lost his school bag, but...

4   I went to Bangalore, but...

5   He is a great swimmer, but...

Top Tip

A comma before 'but' means that the second clause is a contrasting idea.

B

In five of the sentences below the conjunction 'but' should have been used instead of 'and' to join the two clauses together.

Which ones are they?

1   The forecast was for rain and it stayed sunny all day.

2   Mohammed sent in his application for the team and waited for an answer.

3   He was tired and kept working.

4   Maria spent the weekend studying mathematics and writing an essay for English.

5   He is rich and he is not happy.

6   Charlie became addicted to football and that was a surprise to no one.

7   We ordered strawberry ice cream and received vanilla.

8   She bought him a shirt and he hated the colour.

C

Make up three sentences of your own where 'but' is used to indicate a contrast that would not be expected after the first clause. Remember to use a comma before 'but'!

Challenge
Note how 'but' is used by writers of fiction. Is it always used to indicate a contrast?

Words ending in *–er, –or* and *–ar*

Learning objective
Investigate the spellings of word-final unstressed vowels.
Example: The unstressed 'er' at the end of 'butter'.

The endings **–er**, **–or**, and **–ar** can be confused, as they generally sound the same.

▶ **–er** and **–or** endings make nouns which describe someone who performs the action of a verb.

   Examples: To teach = teacher   To garden = gardener

▶ **–er** endings are most common.

▶ **–or** endings are often used for technical and professional nouns.

   Examples: solicitor, professor

 A

Add *–er* or *–or* to the word roots below to make a noun. You might need to use a dictionary to help you.

  a govern_____   **f** spons_____

  b bak_____   **g** dressmak_____

  c edit_____   **h** lawy_____

  d calculat_____   **i** supervis_____

  e protest_____   **j** act_____

 B

–ar as an ending on a noun is fairly rare. Add *–ar* to the examples below. What nouns are formed? Say them out loud, stressing the 'ar' sound.

  a gramm_____

  b burgl_____

  c calend_____

  d cell_____

  e caterpill_____

 C

The adjective ending *–ar* is quite common. Add *–ar* to the examples below. What adjectives are formed?

  a simil_____

  b famili_____

  c peculi_____

  d particul_____

Learning objective
Read and evaluate non-fiction texts for style, clarity and organization.

Word Cloud

country   international
culture   passport
customs   presentation
geography

Home country, what's that?

An interview with a student from the International School of Beijing

Hunter Emigh (aged 10)

Hunter, where do you think of as 'home'?

It's not easy to give an answer to this question. I remember when I was in third grade our teacher asked us to do a research project on our 'home' country and give a presentation. I felt confused. I was born in
5 Texas, USA, but lived in Beijing, China. I liked my school in China, my friends, eating lunch in the big cafeteria, learning how to play a new sport. It felt like home.

Where does your family come from?

My mom says her grandmother was born in Germany, but lives in the
10 USA. My dad says his grandfather was born in Ireland, but lived in France. When I hear the phrase 'home country' I think, what is that? My family come from all over the world.

Nearly all my grandparents had relatives in Germany. I spoke to my grandparents about their childhoods. The more questions I asked them,
15 the more interested I became about how children who live in other countries grow up.

What did you learn from your grandparents?

I learned about children growing up in Germany: how their language was different and how their school holidays were different. Even the
20 geography of their land was different. I learned about German customs like the 'Schultuete', that's a special cone-shaped gift filled with sweets and school supplies that parents give their child on their first day of school.

What did you present for your research project?

25 When it was time for the presentation, my teacher asked me, "Which country are you from?" Even though I was not born there, never lived there, and don't have any living relatives there, I proudly answered, "Germany". Really, I consider myself a person of the world. Maybe next time I'll choose China as my new home country.

What advice would you give to another student who has to move to a new region or country away from what they consider 'home'?

30

My mom says there is an old American saying, "Home is where you hang your hat". I would tell that to friends who
35 have recently moved to a new country. It means that wherever you live you can make a 'home' and identify with the culture and people that live there – no matter what your passport says. My advice would be to embrace the culture you live in. You don't have to forget or leave behind your family
40 history, it's always a part of you wherever you live.

Adapted from *Slurping Soup and Other Confusions:* www.slurpingsoup.com

Comprehension

A

Use words and phrases from the extract to support your answers.

1 Which fact about Hunter is true?

 a Hunter was born in the USA.

 b Hunter doesn't like his school in China.

 c Hunter's grandparents taught him about Chinese customs.

2 Which statement best describes the text?

 a It only contains facts.

 b It has only opinions.

 c It has both facts and opinions.

B

What do you think?

1 Why does Hunter find it difficult to name his 'home country'?

2 Why was Hunter proud to choose Germany?

3 Give a short summary in your own words of the key points in each of Hunter's answers.

4 Write two more questions to ask Hunter that you think would help the reader understand more about his life.

C

What about you?

1 Work with a partner to plan and write an interview about your life at school and where you consider 'home'. Look at the questions in the extract for ideas.

2 Present your interview to the class as a role-play.

Discussion time
"Children should learn about other countries and cultures to help them grow up to be a 'person of the world'." Explain why you agree or disagree.

Pronouns

Learning objective
Use pronouns, making clear to what or to whom they refer.

Pronouns are used in place of nouns. *Examples*: I, me, my, we, our, you, your, she, her, he, him, it, they, their, them

Top Tip

First person can be singular or plural. *Example*: I and we.

A

1 The non-fiction extract *Home country, what's that?* uses lots of different pronouns. Identify six.

2 Why do you think so many pronouns are used in the extract?

  a To make it more personal

  b To make the reader feel more involved

  c It is largely about people and identity

  d To help the reader follow it

The types of pronouns a writer uses can show what point of view the text is being written from...

Point of view	Examples
First person	I, we, me, my, our, us
Second person	you, your
Third person	he, she, it, they, her, him, them, their

B

Look at the table above and answer the question.

The non-fiction extract *Home Country, what's that?* is written in the first person. Are the following sentences written in first, second or third person?

  a I am going home to change my clothes.

  b They are going the wrong way.

  c We spent lunch break playing football.

  d You take 2 kilograms of flour and add to 10 litres of water.

C

Change these sentences from the person in which they are written to either the first or third person.

  a Today it is Monday and I must get ready for school!

  b We take our dog for a walk everyday.

  c They are all going to the cinema.

Silent vowels

Learning objective
Identify silent vowels in polysyllabic words.

Words like 'language' and 'interested' have silent vowels – vowels which are not pronounced. We spell the word like this: 'int/er/est/ed'. But we say the word like this: 'in/trest/ed'.

The red **e** becomes silent – int**e**rested

A

Insert the silent 'e' in the words below.

a veg–table

b temp–rature

c desp–rate

d lit–rature

e cam–ra

B

Find the silent or almost silent letters in the words below.

a hour

b talk

c should

d often

e write

f wrong

Always say the word aloud as you read it to help you think about the 'silent' vowel.

Tricky Spellings

Make a list of words with silent letters that you find difficult. Can you think of a way to remember the silent letters?

C

Choose six words from A and B that you find difficult, and use each one in a sentence. Highlight the silent letter in each case to help you remember them.

Poem about identity

Learning objective
Read poems by significant poets.

Finding a friend

I could not speak your language.
I did not know your rules.
Everything felt foreign
to an alien at school.

Those days are long gone now,
though I thought they'd never end.
Now I have no problems
speaking English, making friends.

Dark and haunting memories
of loneliness and fear,
frustration and confusion
have begun to disappear.

But one thing I'll remember,
one thing will stay the same.
The moment that you smiled at me
and called me by my name.

Jane Clarke

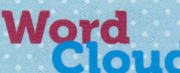

Word Cloud

alien
confusion
foreign
frustration
haunting
moment

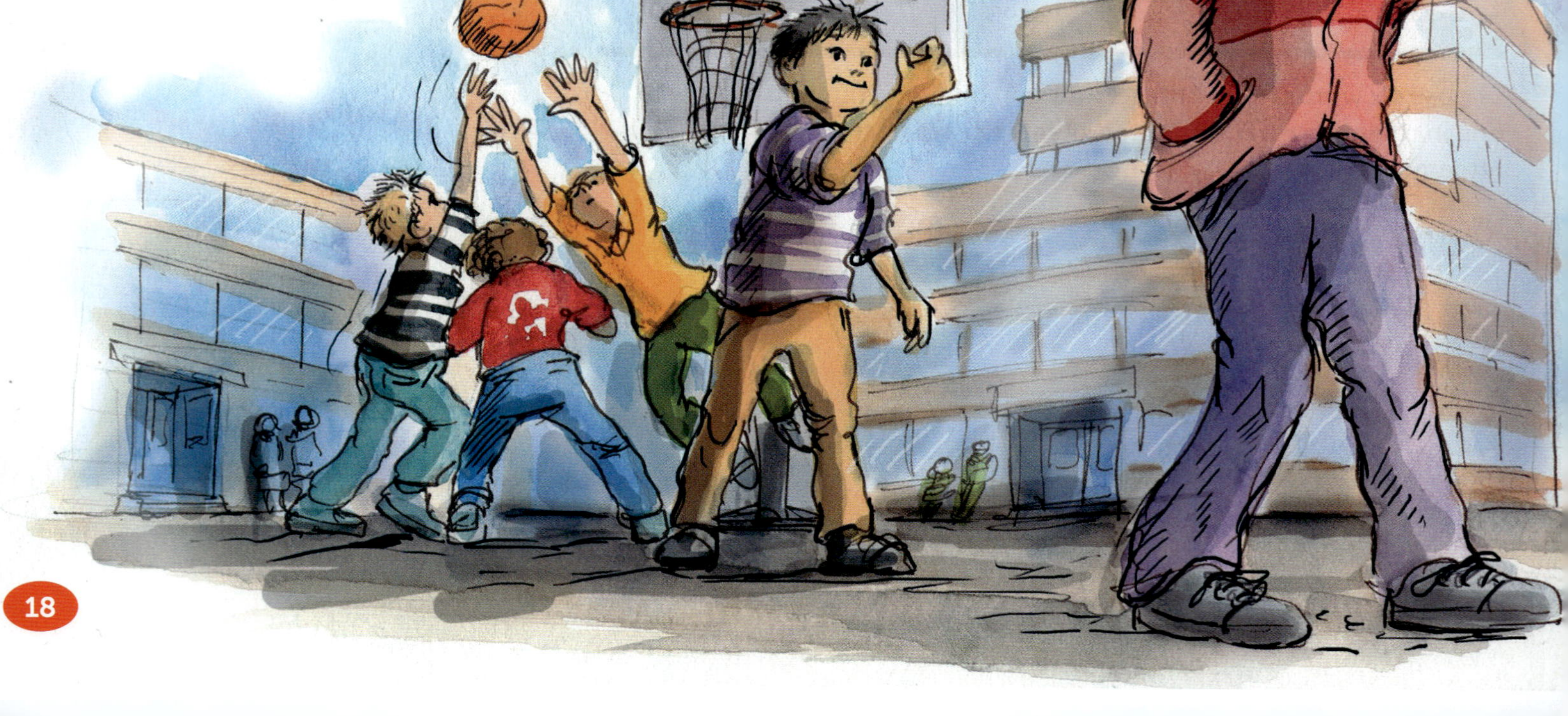

Comprehension

A

Use words or phrases from the poem to support your answers.

1 Which word in verse 1 means 'stranger'?

2 The phrase 'long gone now' in line 5 means:

   a the days at school felt long

   b those days are in the distant past

   c those days are totally forgotten.

3 Which phrase in the last verse talks about a happy memory?

B

Poet's use of language

1 Find eight words used by the poet to show the difficulty of being new in a strange place.

2 What two phrases in verses 2 and 3 show that life is easier for the child now?

3 The poet uses rhyme in alternate lines. List the words that rhyme and explain how this helps the poem.

C

What about you?

1 Which line of the poem do you like best? Explain why.

2 Do you remember a time when you were new to a place or felt like a 'stranger'. What helped you to feel better?

Writing an autobiography

 Learning objective
Mapping out writing to plan structure.

Writing frame
Write about yourself, using the guidelines below.

This is me! I'm happiest when I'm……

swimming…

in the sea at…

feeding my…

at home in the garden…

playing football…

in the park at…

playing ice hockey…

at the ice-rink in…

I feel like a…

The most important people in my life are…

My most precious possession is….

The best thing about my life is…

The strangest thing about my life is…

Sometimes I worry about…

when I'm…

because…

when…

while…

except…

especially…

I'd describe myself as a……

friendly…

noisy…

quiet…

gentle…

outgoing…

confident…

thoughtful…

nervous…

anxious…

easy-going…

jokey…

…kind of person.

Improve your writing

 Learning objective
Choosing words and phrases carefully to convey feeling and atmosphere.

Write about a past event

Write about an event in your past when you felt worried or nervous. It could be when you started a new school or new class or when you moved home.

Questions to help you	Words and phrases you can use
Setting – paragraph 1:	
How old were you?	My most frightening memory happened when I was _____ years old.
Where were you? Describe the place.	I was in/at/beside _____. It was dark/quiet/cold _____ .
What time was it?	I knew it was ___ o'clock because _____ .
Characters – paragraph 2:	
Who were you with?	At the time, I was with _____.
What were they doing?	He/She was _____.
What were you doing?	I was _____ because _____
What happened? – paragraph 3:	
What is the problem?	Just then, /A moment later, /To my surprise, /Suddenly, _____.
How did it get worse?	What was worse, _____ I heard/saw/smelt _____.
Why were you frightened?	I felt as if _____.

2 Food, feasts and festivals

"There is no life I know to compare with pure imagination. Living there, you'll be free if you truly wish to be."
Roald Dahl

Let's Talk

1 Look at the pictures. What foods are they made of?
2 What are your favourite foods?
3 What picture would you create with your favourite foods?

Sound words

Learning objective
Use a thesaurus to extend vocabulary and choice of words.

Some words give you a strong sense or image of the things they describe. *Example*: words like 'scrumptious', 'sticky', 'sweet', 'chocolatey', 'gooey' and 'chewy' are great for describing the taste and texture of a chocolate-and-toffee bar.

You could use any of the words below to describe a delicious food. The underlined words describe texture.

delicious   **nutty**   sweet   **sticky**   **crunchy**   crisp
crackly   fresh   **juicy**   spicy   **creamy**   **soft**

A

1 Say the words out loud to hear them.
2 Take turns to make a sentence using words from above to describe your favourite foods.
   Example: The watermelon was *juicy*, *sweet* and *delicious*.
3 Together match your favourite foods with the words that describe texture above.
   Example: Caramel is my favourite because it is so *sticky*.

In the story, *Charlie and the Chocolate Factory*, the writer, Roald Dahl, uses lots of interesting made-up words like 'Wonka's Whipple-Scrumptious Fudgemallow Delight'. Look at the fantasy lollipops below. Can you imagine how they would taste and feel?

B

Make up a new, unusual sweet and use your dictionary or a thesaurus to help you to describe it.

My fantasy sweet is called _____

It looks like _____

Chocolate fantasy fiction

Learning objective
Identify the point of view from which a story is told.

Charlie Bucket doesn't usually have any money and he is always hungry. He would love to win a ticket to visit the famous Willy Wonka's chocolate factory. One day, he finds a fifty pence coin on the street.

Word Cloud
bulged
extraordinarily
marvellously
wolfing

 ## The Miracle

Charlie entered the shop and laid the damp fifty pence on the counter.

"One Wonka's Whipple-Scrumptious Fudgemallow Delight," he said, remembering how much he had loved the one he had on his
5 birthday.

The man behind the counter looked fat and well-fed. He had big lips and fat cheeks and a very fat neck. The fat around his neck bulged out all around the top of his collar like a rubber ring. He turned and reached behind him for the chocolate bar, then he turned
10 back again and handed it to Charlie. Charlie grabbed it and quickly tore off the wrapper and took an enormous bite. Then he took another …and another …and oh, the joy of being able to fill one's mouth with rich solid food!

"You look like you wanted that one, sonny," the shopkeeper said
15 pleasantly.

Charlie nodded, his mouth bulging with chocolate.

The shopkeeper put Charlie's change on the counter. "Take it easy," he said. "It'll give you a tummy ache if you swallow it like that without chewing."

20 Charlie went on wolfing the chocolate. He couldn't stop. And in less than half a minute, the whole thing had disappeared down his throat. He was quite out of breath, but he felt marvellously, extraordinarily, happy. He reached out a hand to take the change. Then he paused. His eyes were just above the level of the counter.
25 They were staring at the silver coins lying there.

The coins were all five-penny pieces. There were nine of them altogether. Surely it wouldn't matter if he spent just one more…

"I think," he said quietly, "I think… I'll have just one more of those chocolate bars. The same kind as before, please."

30 "Why not?" the fat shopkeeper said, reaching behind him again and taking another Whipple-Scrumptious Fudgemallow Delight from the shelf. He laid it on the counter.

Charlie picked it up and tore off the wrapper… and *suddenly*… from underneath the wrapper… there came a flash of gold.

35 Charlie's heart stood still.

"It's a Golden Ticket!" screamed the shopkeeper, leaping about a foot in the air. "You've got a Golden Ticket! You've found the last Golden Ticket! Hey, would you believe it! Come and look at this everybody! The kid's found Wonka's last Golden Ticket! There it is!
40 It's right here in his hands!"

From *Charlie and the Chocolate Factory* by Roald Dahl

Comprehension

 A

Give evidence from the extract in your answers for A and B.

1 What was Charlie's favourite sweet called?
2 How did Charlie feel when he had swallowed the chocolate bar?
3 What did Charlie decide to do instead of taking his change?
4 What did Charlie see under the wrapper? Why did the writer use this phrase?

 B

What do you think?

1 Do you think that Charlie had chocolate very often?
2 After he found the ticket, what do you think happened next to Charlie?
3 Write one sentence which sums up Charlie's feelings, and another sentence to sum up the shopkeeper's feelings.

 C

What about you?

Have you ever won something? How did you feel?

Glossary

change the money returned after buying something

counter the sales surface in a shop

fifty pence, five-penny pieces UK coins

foot a measurement equal to 30.5cm

one's belonging to or a person's

sonny friendly name for a boy

Direct speech

Learning objective
Begin to set out dialogue appropriately, using a range of punctuation.

▶ Speech marks like this **" "** go before and after words spoken by a person in a text. They help to show who is talking.
Example: **"**You look like you wanted that one, sonny**,"** the shopkeeper said.

▶ A new line should start every time a new person speaks.
Example: **"**What would you like, sonny**?"** asked the shopkeeper.
           "I'll have two chocolate bars, please**,"** said Charlie.

▶ A capital letter is used for the opening word of a speech.

▶ A comma is used before the speech marks close.
Example: **"**I feel marvellously happy**,"** said Charlie.

▶ Some sentences need a question mark or an exclamation mark. These go inside the speech marks.
Example: **"**What would you like**?"** asked the shopkeeper.
           "He's won**!"** the man shouted.

▶ The reporting clause, like *the shopkeeper said,* can come at the start, middle or end of the sentence. *Example:* **"**Take it easy**," he said, "**it'll give you a tummy ache.**"** (middle)

 A

Put speech marks and correct punctuation in these sentences.

1 The boy said. He's won the golden ticket.

2 Do you know where Mr Wonka's factory is I said.

3 I'm not sure which way to go said Charlie.

4 You'll get a sore tummy if you eat it all at once said Mr Wonka.

 B

Turn the sentences above around so that 'said' is in a different place.

Example: "He's won the golden ticket!" **the boy said.**

 C

In the dialogue below change the word 'said' to one of the words in blue. Put in correct punctuation.

shouted whispered screamed asked explained

Charlie picked up the chocolate bar and tore off the wrapper …and suddenly there came a flash of gold. What is that <u>said</u> the shopkeeper

I think it's a Golden Ticket, to visit Mr Wonka's chocolate factory <u>said</u> Charlie Hey, <u>said</u> the shopkeeper would you believe it, you've won he <u>said</u>.

Challenge
Create and write down your own dialogue, set in a sweet shop with two characters talking. Practise speaking your dialogue with a partner.

Suffixes

Learning objectives
Understand and use the correct spelling rules for –y endings.
Use the suffix –ful to change a root word into an adjective.

- A suffix is one letter or a group of letters that can be added to the end of a word.
- You can add the suffix **–ful** to the end of a word to change it to an adjective.
  Example: I need some **help** with my homework.
  I found a help**ful** website when I was studying.
- When a word ends with **y** change the **y** into **i**.
  Example: beaut**y**   beaut**i**ful
- Use the suffix **–al** to change a noun to an adjective.
  Example: logic   logic**al**
- When a noun ends in an **e** remove it before adding the suffix **–al**.
  Example: approv**e**   approv**al**

A

Choose the correct word and add the *–ful* suffix to turn it into an adjective.

peace   wonder   duty   plenty   skill

1 My friend is a _____ basketball player.
2 The tree gave us a _____ supply of juicy apples.
3 My grandparents tell me to be a _____ son and help with the chores and study hard.
4 Our class had a _____ trip to the museum last week.
5 The lunch area was quiet and _____ today because three classes were on a school trip.

B

Add the *–ful* suffix to these words and write your own sentences.

**thought   joy   tear   help   thank   waste   rest
pain   colour**

Example: We had a **restful** holiday by the sea last year.

C

Add the *–al* suffix to these words, remembering the 'e' spelling rule.
Write your own sentences.

**addition   sensation   bride   spine   tropic
tone   season   tradition   medic   nation**

Example: The men came to remov**e** all our furniture when we moved house. Their remov**al** truck blocked the road for a few hours.

Challenge
With a partner use a dictionary to find as many new *–ful* and *–al* words as you can and then test each other on the spelling and meaning of the words.

The origins of Chocolate

Chocolate is made from cacao. The Maya of Mexico discovered cacao as long ago as 600 CE. They picked cacao from the wild trees and then began to plant them specially. The Aztec people became powerful after the Maya.

5 They were very fond of chocolatl, a drink made from roasted beans and water with hot chilli to make it spicy. They poured the chocolatl from a great height to make it go frothy! Mexicans still make their hot chocolate frothy today.

Precious beans

Cacao beans were so valuable that they were used as money.
10 A rabbit cost ten beans and a pumpkin cost four. They were also used in important ceremonies and traded for cloth, jade and ceremonial feathers.

A cacao tree produces between 20 and 30 pods a year. Pods from one tree would make 450 grams of chocolate
15 powder, about the same as a small bag of sugar. There are about 20 to 40 beans in each pod.

Powder to bars

Soon people began to add milk to the chocolate, but it was still only a drink. Then, from about 1850, factories began to manufacture and sell cocoa powder in tins and this led to chocolate bars. Mexican women used to press cocoa powder
20 into blocks so that they could keep it. But it wasn't sweet like modern chocolate bars.

Health food

Today people like chilli chocolate, just like the Aztecs, and it is a very fashionable flavour. Doctors say that pure chocolate is good for us, because it contains important
25 vitamins, but only a little at a time! Too much sweetened chocolate can rot teeth and be fattening.

Glossary

Aztec people members of the civilization that was dominant in Mexico before the Spanish Conquest of the sixteenth century

CE Common Era

Maya an ancient Indian civilization from Central America from about 1000 CE

Pods from a cacao tree

Comprehension

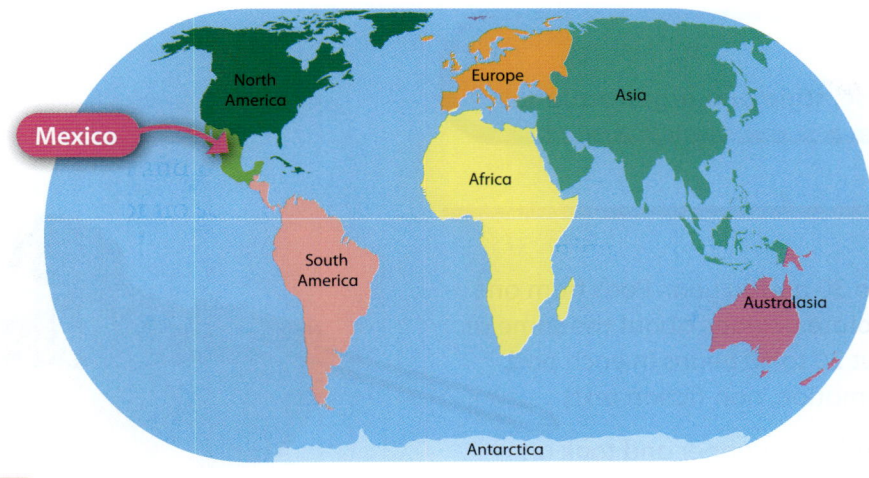

Using a molinillo to whisk chocolate

Give evidence from the extract to support your answers.

1 Who were the first people to discover cacao?

2 What were cacao beans used for?

A molinillo from Mexico

What do you think?

1 The pods from one cacao tree produce 20 grams of chocolate powder. True or false?

2 Chocolatl was a drink made with sugar. True or false?

3 Pure chocolate is unhealthy. True or false?

Discussion time
Is chocolate bad or good for us? Research and debate.

What about you?

1 What foods do you eat on special occasions like birthdays?

2 Think about two festivals in your country and the food eaten during that time.

3 Describe a festival to a partner and include: how long it lasts, the time of year, and the type of food you eat.

Challenge
Do you know the history of your festival foods?

When were they first eaten and how were they prepared?

Did they come from your country or a different country?

29

Language for information texts

Learning objective
Evaluate non-fiction text for purpose, style and organization.

A

Read the sentences below.

A cacao tree produces between 20 to 30 pods a year. Pods from one tree would make 450 grams of chocolate powder, about the same as a small bag of sugar. There are about 20 to 40 beans in each pod. ('The Origins of Chocolate' – an information, non-fiction text)

Charlie grabbed it and quickly tore off the wrapper and took an enormous bite… He was quite out of breath, but he felt marvellously, extraordinarily, happy.
(*Charlie and the Chocolate Factory* – a fantasy narrative fiction text)

B

Complete the table with examples from the extracts to show the types of words and features used in each text.

Types of word	*The Origins of Chocolate*	*Charlie and the Chocolate Factory*
Personal pronouns	none	he
Characters' names		
Adjectives		
Adverbs		
Numbers		
Subheadings		
Direct speech		

Top Tips

▶ Non-fiction writers often want to explain a process or an historical event.
▶ They use shorter sentences, and include more numbers and dates.

C

1   What is the purpose of the information text, 'The Origins of Chocolate'? What does the writer want to achieve?
2   What is the purpose of the fantasy fiction text, 'Charlie and the Chocolate Factory'? What does the author want to communicate to the reader?

Challenge
Read a different non-fiction text and list all the features.

Adverbs

An **adverb** is a word which gives more information about a verb.

Examples:
How? 'The student answered **politely**.
When? She played the piano **today**.
Where? The teachers are talking **downstairs**.

Many 'how' adverbs put **–ly** on the end of an adjective.

Example: Charlie... quick**ly** tore off the chocolate wrapper
The verb action 'tore' is described by the adverb.

When an adjective ends in the letter **y** remove the 'y' and add **–ily** to turn it into an adverb.

 A

Change these adjectives into adverbs by adding *–ly* or *–ily*.

lazy silent happy scary marvellous

B

Are the adverbs below telling you how, when or where?

1 outside

2 tomorrow

3 cheerfully

4 yesterday

5 quickly

6 somewhere

7 before

8 lazily

 C

Complete each of these sentences with a different adverb.

1 The student whispered _____.

2 The children played football _____.

3 The boy ate his food _____.

4 The children are playing _____.

5 The girl jumped and laughed _____.

Remember an adjective describes a noun. An adverb describes a verb.

Poem

 Learning objective
Explore the form and themes of a poem and interpret the style, imagery and language chosen by the poet.

Word Cloud
pounding
sounding

The poet Afua Cooper lives in Canada, but she comes from Jamaica.

 Kensington Market

Colours
Colours
Colours everywhere
colours of food
5   and
colours of people
music sounding
music pounding
Kensington Market on a Saturday morning.

10 Every Saturday morning
Mom takes her shopping basket
and we go to Kensington Market
Bananas
yams
15 pumpkin
mangos
okras
and
'whappen'!*
20 Caribbean scent.

* 'Whappen!' means
'It's all happening'.

Afua Cooper

Comprehension

A

Give evidence from the poem in your answers for A and B.

1 What things does the poet see in the market?
2 What is the word the poet uses most and why?
3 Which lines only have one word?

B

What do you think?

1 What effect do the lines with only one word have on the way the poem is read?
2 Why do you think Afua likes this market so much?
3 Why does she use some of the words more than once?
4 Which senses does the poet include?

C

What about you?

1 Have you been to a food market? Describe it to a partner.
2 With a partner, write a new verse for the poem using the senses of smell, touch and taste.

Festival recount

Learning objective
Use a more specialized vocabulary to match a topic.

Model Writing

Children's Day in Mexico

In Mexico Children's Day is on 30 April. Children and teachers go to school but nobody really works!

Everybody dresses up brightly and the teachers decorate the school with candles and balloons. It is one of the happiest days of the year. Children play games like 'Pin the tail on the donkey' and get toys and sweets. It's a lively party with delicious food, puppet shows and fairgrounds.

The best part of the festival for me is that we get to dress up. In the photo, I'm wearing the national costume of Mexico.

Write a personal recount

Think about the festivals you discussed on page 29. Choose one festival and write three very short paragraphs about it. Include a description of festival food using the words you learnt on pages 23 and 29.

Plan your writing using these questions and answers to help you.

What is the topic?	A festival
What is the purpose?	To explain what happens during the festival
What kind of non-fiction text will you write?	Information text in the first person *Example*: I decorated the...
What features will be used?	Drawing or photo Title, subheadings

Use the questions in the three balloons below to help you to write each paragraph.

Paragraph 1
Introduction

What is the name of the festival?

Where is the festival celebrated (name of country or city)?

When in the year does it take place?

Who is involved in celebrating it?

Paragraph 2
Main

How is the festival celebrated?

Describe the clothes, food, games or activities.

Paragraph 3
Conclusion

What is your favourite part of the festival? Describe it and explain why you like it.

3 Our blue planet

Arctic Ocean

Atlantic
Ocean

Pacific
Ocean

Pacific
Ocean

Indian
Ocean

> **"I'm not afraid of storms for I'm learning how to sail my ship."**
> Louisa May Alcott

Let's Talk

1 Look at the oceans on the map. Water covers nearly three-quarters of the Earth's surface. Count the number of oceans on the map.

2 What do you think this unit is about? How do you know?

3 Have you seen a storm at sea? If so, tell a partner about it.

4 Do you think Louisa May Alcott believes we should always keep safe or learn how to look after ourselves?

Describing the sea

On this page you will learn some exciting verbs that help you to imagine storms at sea. Verbs are 'doing words' so they tell you what the sea **does**. *Example*: it **roars** and **pounds** on the beach.

Match the word to its meaning

A

Match each word to its meaning. Use a dictionary to help you.

Example: **1** crashing: **c** making a loud noise

1	crashing	**a**	moving in a curve
2	curling	**b**	beating down
3	exploding	**c**	making a loud noise
4	lashing	**d**	moving like a whip
5	pounding	**e**	moving something up and down very fast
6	shaking	**f**	falling
7	tumbling	**g**	bursting with a loud noise

Because there is so much water on Earth, it is sometimes called 'The Blue Planet'.

B

Rewrite the sentences below, replacing the underlined words with a word from the list of words in blue.

vast din awestruck fearsome battering

Example: The boy watched the **vast** waves.

1 The sea was <u>hitting</u> the ship.

2 He was <u>amazed</u> by the scene.

3 He heard the <u>noise</u> of the water crashing against the boat.

4 A <u>scary</u> creature appeared out of nowhere.

Which sentences sound more interesting – those with the underlined words or the new ones you have written?

An adventure story

Learning objective

Comment on a writer's use of language and explain reasons for the writer's choices.

Michael, a 12-year-old boy, has been sailing around the world with his parents in a boat called the *Peggy Sue*. In a fierce storm, Michael and his dog Stella were washed into the sea. They are now on a desert island but it seems that they are not alone.

Word Cloud
huddled
roared
rolling
spread

Storm at Sea

A storm broke over the island that night, such a fearsome storm, such a thunderous crashing of lightning overhead, such a din of rain and wind that sleep was quite impossible. Great waves roared in from the ocean, pounding the beach, and shaking the ground beneath me. I spread out my
5   sleeping mat at the very back of the cave. Stella lay down beside me and huddled close. How I welcomed that.

It was fully four days before the storm blew itself out, but even during the worst of it, I would find my fish and fruit breakfast waiting for me every morning under my tin, which he had now wedged tight in under the same
10   shelf of rock. Stella and I kept to the shelter of our cave. All we could do was watch as the rain came lashing down outside. I looked on awestruck at the power of the vast waves rolling in from the open sea, curling, tumbling, and exploding as they broke onto the beach, as if they were trying to batter the island into pieces and then suck us all
15   out to sea. I thought often of my mother and father and the *Peggy Sue*, and wondered where they were. I just hoped the typhoon – for that was what I was witnessing – had passed them by.

From *Kensuke's Kingdom* by Michael Morpurgo

Comprehension

A

Give evidence from the extract in your answers.

1 When did the storm break out?
2 Who was with Michael on the island?
3 How long did the storm last?
4 What did Michael have to eat?

B

What do you think?

1 Why does Michael stay inside the cave?
2 Why couldn't Michael fall asleep?
3 Michael thought about his parents. Where do you think they were?
4 How does the writer describe the waves in lines 12 and 13 and why does he use this language?

C

What about you?

1 Retell the story extract in your own words to a partner.
2 What is the first thing you would do if you found yourself on a remote island? Give a reason to explain your actions to your partner.

Glossary

remote far from anywhere else

typhoon a very strong storm at sea

witnessing watching

Similes and metaphors

Learning objective
Discuss metaphorical expressions and figures of speech.

Writers often use **similes** and **metaphors** to create an 'extra' image for the reader, so that they can see and imagine better.

Examples: The wind whipped round my ankles like an angry dog. (simile)

Her home was a prison. (metaphor)

A

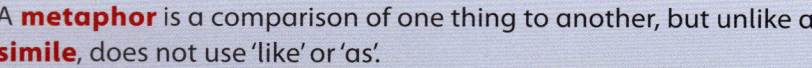

A simile is always introduced by the words 'like' or 'as'.

Complete the following similes.

   a The night was as dark as ___.

   b Like ___, the aeroplane rose in the air.

   c The sea was as angry as ___.

   d Her legs shook like ___.

   e Paint spilled on to the road like ___.

A **metaphor** is a comparison of one thing to another, but unlike a **simile**, does not use 'like' or 'as'.

Example: He is like a bright light (simile).
He is the bright light of the school. (metaphor)

B

Identify which of these comparisons is a simile or a metaphor.

   a I was as angry as a crazed tiger.

   b The teeth of crocodiles are white daggers.

   c The fog enveloped us like a thick, grey duvet.

   d The moon is a giant football in the sky.

   e The room was as untidy as the inside of the school wastepaper bin.

C

Write a paragraph about a storm – either on land or at sea. Include the storm beginning, then getting worse and gradually dying out. Use at least two similes and two metaphors.

Challenge
Keep an on-going list of effective similes and metaphors used by writers.

Adding –*ing*

Learning objective
Learn spelling rules for words ending in –e and –y and know rules for doubling consonants.

When adding the suffix **–ing** to a word, the following rules apply.

▶ If the root word ends in –e, remove it before adding **–ing**.
Example: tak**ing**.

▶ If the vowel sound of the root word is short, and ends in a consonant, double the letter before adding **–ing**.
Example: ge**tting**.

▶ If neither of these apply, generally just add **–ing**.
Example: happen**ing**.

 A

Complete the table.

Root word	–ing added	
break		
	pounding	
roll		
	crashing	
rumble		
	exploding	
run		

 B

Find the five errors made with the adding of –*ing* in the writing below. How would you correct these errors?

I was runing so quickly that everything was droping out of my rucksack. I noticed my jacket was also dragging on the floor. I was in such a hurry! I only had half an hour left to get to the rideing stables to get ready for the race. Would we make a wining team? I knew that as soon as I saw my horse I would be huging him – just for luck.

 C

You should now be familiar with the spelling rule for adding –*ing*. Make a small poster or 'help card' which explains it to other students.

Life in the sea

Learning objective
Develop note-taking to extract key points and to group and link ideas.

Life in the sea

Life on Earth began in the sea millions of years ago. The first living things were far smaller than the dot on this i. As millions of years passed, thousands of different sea plants and animals took on many shapes, sizes and colours. Some began to swim, some began to crawl. Some are
5   still around today and some are not.

Dead and gone

Trilobites were among the earliest animals and lived in the sea more than 510 million years ago. They had jointed legs and external skeletons like insects and crabs. We don't know why, but about 250 million years ago they all died out, so trilobites became extinct. We only know about
10   them because some of their remains turned into stones called fossils. Scientists use the fossils to work out how long ago they lived.

Still here today

The brittle star is a sea creature that is luckier than the trilobite! This 180-million-year-old fossil looks like its living relative. Brittle stars have a round central disc and five fragile jointed arms that can easily
15   break. Today, as in the past, large numbers of them are often found on sandy or muddy sea beds.

Why do some animals become extinct?

So why did the trilobite become extinct and why did the brittle star survive until the twenty-first century? After all, the trilobites lived on Earth for about 270 million years – a hundred times as long as
20   human beings! Is it because something happened to their food chain?

Food chains

All plants and animals in the sea are part of a food chain. Plants produce their own food from sunlight. This is why they are called the 'producers' in a food chain. Animals can't produce their own
25   food – they need to consume other animals or plants to survive. This is why animals are called consumers. Plant-eating animals are called 'primary consumers', or herbivores, and meat-eating animals are called 'secondary' and 'tertiary' consumers, or carnivores. If they kill other animals, we also call them predators.

Glossary
brittle easy to break
external on the outside
extinct not alive now
fossils hardened remains of plants or animals
survive continue to live

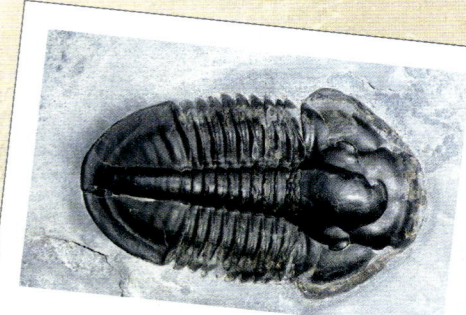

A trilobite

A brittle star

30 Here is an example of a food chain at sea.

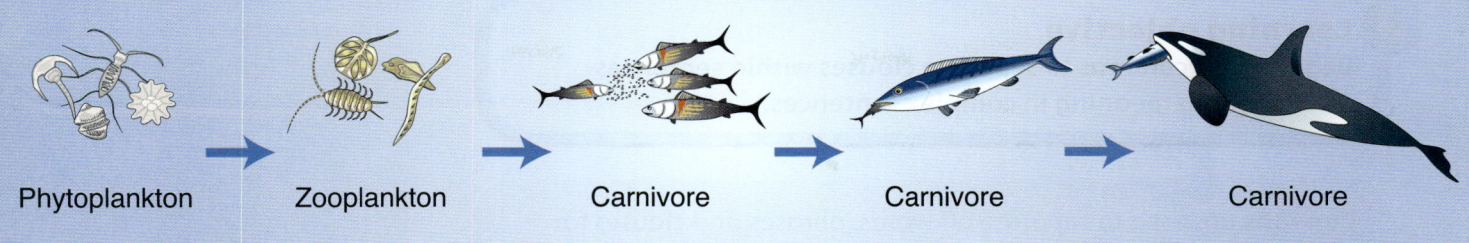

Phytoplankton → Zooplankton → Carnivore → Carnivore → Carnivore

If the producers die, the consumers are also in danger because the producers (such as phytoplankton) provide the energy in their food chain. Scientists tell us that many different kinds of plants and animals became extinct 250 million years ago – at the same time as the trilobites. Perhaps
35 trilobites died out because something happened to destroy their food chain.

Comprehension

A

Give short answers.

1 Where did the first living things live? *Example*: In the sea.

2 Name two features of a trilobite.

3 Name an animal that lived more than a million years ago and can still be found today.

4 What happens to the animals in a food chain if the plants die?

B

Choose the correct word in each sentence.

1 Plants **consume/produce** their own food from water and sunlight, so they are called **consumers/producers**.

2 Next in the food chain are zooplankton, which are very tiny animals. They eat the diatoms, so they are **consumers/producers**. Another name for them is **herbivores/carnivores**.

3 Crabs then eat the zooplankton, so they are both **consumers/producers** and **herbivores/carnivores**.

C

What about you?

1 What do you think was the main point of each of the five paragraphs in the extract? Write five sentences, one for each main point.

2 Where do you think humans fit into the marine food chain? How might we be responsible for the extinction of marine plants and animals?

Humans are consumers of fish.

43

Commas

Learning objective

Begin to use commas to separate clauses within sentences and to clarify meaning in complex sentences.

Commas are used to separate off words, phrases and clauses for the reader.

 A

In the non-fiction text, *Life in the Sea*, the writer has used commas in different ways.

Find and copy out examples of a comma used:

1 before the conjunction 'but'

2 after a clause beginning with 'If'

3 after a clause beginning with 'As'

4 after a time word or connective.

 B

Insert the five commas that have been left out in the extract below.

As I made my way back home I felt a sudden flicker of unease. Were those dark clouds above me? If there was going to be a storm I would be soaked. I only had on a T-shirt but I did have a thin jacket in my bag. Also I had a hat. The sky brightened. Today it was going to be my lucky day.

Pairs of commas are also used to separate, or chunk off, a clause or phrase in the middle of a sentence.

Example: The waves **,** which were the biggest I had ever seen **,** rolled over the town.

 C

Drop the following clauses and phrases into the middle of the sentence, remembering to use the pairs of commas!

1 The plates were brought in by my mother. (which were heaped with food)

2 Emmanuel shot the ball into the net. (with a flick of his heel)

3 From there Fatima could see the old castle quite clearly. (lying half buried in the leaves)

4 I thought the dress was exquisite. (the silver one with gold stripes)

5 Petra strolled in and hung up her coat. (who was a tall girl)

Challenge
Keep a track of the different ways you use commas in your own writing. You could even keep a tally in columns at the back of your exercise book.

Connectives

> **Learning objective**
> Investigate clauses within sentences and how they are connected.

In a non-fiction information text like *Life in the Sea*, **subordinating connectives** are important because they link and explain points precisely.

A

How many times are these subordinating connectives used in 'Life in the Sea'?

Subordinating connective	Number of times used
If	
As	
because	
so	
that	

B

1 Rewrite this sentence from the extract, replacing 'because' with 'and'.

   'Perhaps tribolites died out **because** something happened to destroy their food chain.'

   What difference does changing 'because' make?

2 Rewrite this sentence from the extract, replacing 'If' with 'As'.

   '**If** they kill other animals, we call them predators.'

   What difference does changing 'If' make?

C

Extend the simple sentences below by using one of these connectives.

that   so   because   if   as

1 Tigers are fast.
2 We will go the sports shop.
3 She wore a dress.
4 I will go.
5 The hat was big.

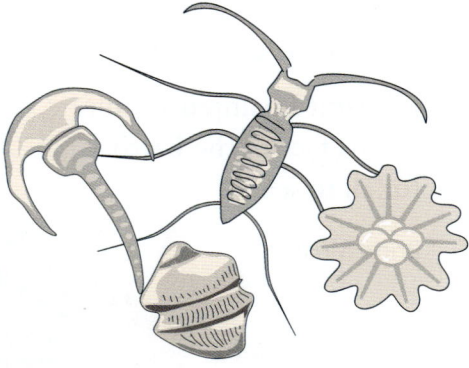

Phytoplankton

A dream poem

Brian Moses is a children's poet who lives in England but also travels around Europe reading his poems to children.

Word Cloud

blackened	poisoned
dreamer	polluted
ivory	

 ## Dreamer

I dreamt I was an ocean
and no one polluted me.

I dreamt I was a whale
and no hunter chased after me.

5 I dreamt I was the air
and nothing blackened me.

I dreamt I was a stream
and nobody poisoned me.

I dreamt I was an elephant
10 and nobody stole my ivory.

I dreamt I was a rainforest
and no one cut down my trees.

I dreamt I painted a smile
on the face of the Earth
15 for all to see.

Brian Moses

46

Comprehension

A

1 **Match each verse to its illustration.**

Example: **1 B**

2 **Complete the sentences.**

The poet dreams that:

a the rainforests aren't being destroyed in verse ___.

b the world isn't being polluted in verses ___, ___ and
___ ___.

B

What do you think?

1 Why do you think the poet repeats the same words in each verse?

2 How do you think we can paint 'a smile on the face of the Earth'?

C

What about you?

1 Do you feel that the Earth is in danger from pollution and the destruction of its wildlife and rainforests?

2 Find out about one of the environmental dangers to the country you live in. These could be:

- pollution
- climate change
- wildlife extinction
- building on fields and forests.

Tell the rest of the group what you found out, and what your feelings are about it.

Challenge

Have you ever dreamt you were somebody else? Or something else? Tell your partner about a dream you have had. Then read about Brian Moses' dreams.

Discussion time

List four ways that we can make the Earth a better place to live. In a group compare your lists and pick the top idea.

Write an adventure story

Learning objective

Map out writing to plan a story structure with a setting, two characters, a problem, suspense and a resolution.

You are going to write an adventure story about a sea rescue. Most good adventures have:

- ▶ a setting (which helps the reader to imagine where and when it happened)
- ▶ characters (the people in the story)
- ▶ a problem (something that goes wrong)
- ▶ suspense (which makes the reader want to find out what happened next)
- ▶ a resolution (which tells you how the problem was solved).

Writing frame – Sea rescue!

YOU are the main character! Imagine walking by the sea one day. You see someone in the sea….. Use the writing frame to help you, but use your own ideas too.

Questions to think about	Useful phrases
Setting Where and when did it happen?	It was…
Characters Who did you see in the sea? What was he / she doing? What did the person look like?	All of a sudden / To my surprise / To my horror I saw / noticed / heard He / She was waving / shouting / holding a rope He / She had grey hair / a yellow jacket / a blue hat
Problem Where was the person? Why did the person need help?	near / far from / way out a boat / the shore / the rocks no life jacket / a long way out / couldn't swim
Suspense What were the dangers? Why was it difficult for you?	tide coming up / a shark approaching / waves getting higher / boat drifting away too far to swim / heavy clothes / freezing water / no life jacket / no mobile phone / no boat
Resolution How did you rescue him / her?	Suddenly I remembered / noticed / realized… At last / Eventually / To my relief…

Write a sea narrative story

Your writing

Write the opening paragraph of a story set EITHER by a rough sea OR by a calm sea.

Use this writing frame to give you ideas, but use your own ideas too.

Example: It was a cool evening in March. I was walking…

It was a	Sunday morning in December. cool evening in March. lazy afternoon in July.
I was walking	beside the rocks on my way to… near the beach because… along the cliff to find…
The sea	was sparkling in the sun. was crashing against the rocks. was…
The lapping waves The tumbling waves The… waves	sounded like…

Top Tip

Remember the similes and metaphors from page 40? Use some in your writing so that your reader can clearly imagine the scene you're describing.

Revise and check ❶

Vocabulary

1 Make a list of the words in the phrases below which have a silent letter. Circle the silent letter of each word. Write a sentence for each phrase.

   a chilli chocolate

   b correct answers

   c rustling papers

   d low temperatures

   e vegetable curry.

2 Choose a better word than 'said' in these sentences. Use words from the list below.

   shouted asked screamed explained

   a "Is there a storm coming?" the boy said.

   b "There are always storms here in October," said the Captain.

   c "Hey! Be careful!" he said to the boy.

   d "Oh no!" said the boy, as the wave hit.

3 Answer these questions on metaphor:

   a Does this metaphor describe a storm or a cacao tree?

     'an orchestra of drums and trumpets'

   b Give reasons for your answer.

   c Write a metaphor to describe your favourite fruit.

Punctuation

1 Add the correct punctuation to this passage:

That afternoon Maya decided to go to the market. As she approached she could smell the different fruit. There were bananas pineapples and mangoes but the melon seller wasn't there. If he was going to come he would be behind the orange tree. His juicy ripe fruit was the best and his cheerful face with the friendly smile was like a ray of sunshine.

Is the melon seller coming today asked Maya.

I am not sure answered the old woman but he is often late on Tuesdays.

Grammar

1 Complete the table with the adjective or adverb. Choose a word from the table to complete the sentences below.

Adjective	Adverb
cheerful	_____
_____	quickly
polite	_____
_____	happily
silent	

They welcomed the new girl c_____. She was s_____ at first but then answered their questions p_____. She didn't make friends q_____ but by the end of the week she looked h_____.

Spelling

1 Choose the correct ending to make nouns.

–or   –ar   –er

a lawy____

b burgl____

c govern____

d caterpill____

2 Turn the words into adjectives by writing the words with the correct suffix.

–al   or   –ful

a help

b tradition

c thought

d waste

e nation

f spine

Explain the rule when the word ends in an 'e'

3 Add the suffix **–ing** to the root words in brackets.

They heard the waves (explode), and (hit) the side of the ship. Thunder was (roar) and (rumble) in the distance and there was no sign of the storm (stop).

4 Stories and comic strips

"There's something you need to know about failure, Tintin. You can never let it defeat you."

Hergé

Let's Talk

1 Look at the three comic strips. Which do you like best? Explain why.

2 Do you think reading cartoon stories is better than reading ordinary fiction stories? Explain your opinion to a partner.

Cartoons as stories

🌍 **Learning objective**
Identify unfamiliar words and explore definitions.

Word Cloud

artwork	hero
cartoon	illustrator
champion	magazine
comic strip	manga
drama	pirate
falconer	

A

Match the descriptions with the three comic strips.

1 Tintin, the hero, is a Belgian newspaper reporter. Snowy, his white dog, and his friend Captain Haddock help him on his adventures. The story of Tintin was first written and illustrated as books in French and then became an animated film.

2 Sultan's dream is to become a champion falconer in the Gold Ring competition. The Manga stories about him come from the United Arab Emirates.

3 The *Pirates of Pangaea* appears in a weekly British magazine called *Phoenix*. The story of Sophie Delacourt continues week by week.

B

Tell a partner about a heroic character from a story or comic that you have read.

My favourite hero/heroine is _____

I like him/her because _____

C

Fiction

> **Learning objective**
> Read widely and explore the features of different fiction genres.

Alfie likes to escape to his private world in the attic to draw cartoons. He dreams that one day he and his attic will be famous.

The Cartoonist

"Did you hear me, Alfie?"

Alfie didn't answer. He was drawing a comic strip called 'Super Bird'.

In the first square a man was scattering birdseed from a bag
5   labelled 'Little Bird Seed'. In the next square little birds were gobbling up the seeds. In the third square the man was scattering bird seed from a bag labelled 'Big Bird Seed.' In the next square big birds were gobbling up the seeds. In the fifth square the man was scattering huge lumps from a bag labelled 'Giant Bird Seed'. In the last square a
10   giant bird was gobbling up the little man.

There was a smile on Alfie's face as he looked at what he had done. At the top of the drawing he lettered in the words *Super Bird*. He was going to do twelve of these super comic strips, he decided, one for each month. He would call it 'Super Calendar'. Maybe he would get
15   it published, and later, when he learned how, he would animate

Word Cloud

attic
lettered
published
scattering

'Super Bird', and make it into a film. Whenever he drew something, he always saw it in motion.

"Alfie?" his mom called again. "Supper is ready. Come down right now..."

20 Alfie knew she was at the foot of the ladder now. She rattled the ladder as if she were trying to shake him down. "I'm coming up there to pull you down by the ear if you don't come this minute."

"I'm coming."

He got up quickly and turned his papers face down on the table. He
25 started for the ladder that led downstairs.

Coming down from the attic was like getting off one of those rides at the amusement park, Alfie thought. It left him feeling strange, as if he had moved not from one part of the house to another but from one experience to another without time to get his balance.

Adapted from *The Cartoonist* by Betsy Byars

Comprehension

Learning objective
Comment on the writer's use of language and explain reasons for writer's choices.

 A

Give evidence from the extract in your answers to A and B.

1 What was Alfie doing when his mother called him?
2 What was the name of his comic strip?
3 How many pictures are in Alfie's comic strip?

B

What do you think?

1 Why didn't Alfie go down for supper immediately?
2 How do you know that Alfie's mom was angry?
3 Why did coming down from the attic leave Alfie feeling strange?

 C

What about you?

1 Create a storyboard for this extract from *The Cartoonist*. Draw the different parts of the story and label them 1 to 6 so that they are in the correct order.
2 In your own words, write a sentence for each of the six scenes you have made. These sentences will summarize each part of the story.

Glossary

animate to give life to

calendar a year planner

comic strip several cartoons which tell a story mostly in pictures

mom American for 'mother'

Modifying adverbs

Learning objective
Extend understanding of the use of adverbs to qualify verbs. Example: in dialogue.

Adverbs modify and add information to a verb. They are often formed by adding the suffix **–ly** to the root word.

Example: quick – quickly

Adverbs are useful in dialogues because they give information on how a person speaks.

A

Add one of these adverbs to each of the sentences below.

excitedly   thoughtfully   patiently   quietly   sharply

1 "SSh! We mustn't make any noise," she whispered _____.

2 "Sit down, right now!" the head teacher shouted _____.

3 "Let me explain it you," the teacher said _____.

4 "Mmmm...You have a good point there," she said _____.

5 "We've won!" she screamed _____.

B

Here are two pieces of dialogue. Write them out again, adding a suitable *–ly* adverb in the space.

"Alfie?" his mom called again _____. "Supper is ready. Come down right now".

"Alfie, what are you doing up there?" his mom called _____ .
"I want to talk to you!"

C

Write eight separate dialogue sentences of your own. Use a different adverb from the list below for each sentence to describe how the person speaks.

slowly   anxiously   cheerfully   furiously
kindly   politely   rudely   suddenly

Example: "Don't move," she said **slowly**. "I think there's somebody in the house."

Top Tip
When writing dialogues, consider adding *–ly* adverbs.

Prepositions

Learning objective

Identify prepositions and use the term.

Prepositions are short words that show relationship, position or movement. *Examples*: with, in, to

  A

Find the seven prepositions in the extract below from *The Cartoonist*. The first one has been underlined.

There was a smile <u>on</u> Alfie's face as he looked at what he had done. At the top of the drawing he lettered the words 'Super Bird'. He was going to do twelve of these super comic strips, he decided, one for each month. He would call it 'Super Calendar'. Maybe he would get it published, and later, when he had learned how, he could animate 'Super Bird', and make it into a film.

Some prepositions can be used for both position and movement.
Example: He put the keys **in** his pocket. There was no money **in** the box.

Some prepositions are generally used for movement, not position.
Example: They quickly got **out of** the bus.

  B

Work in pairs. Choose the correct preposition of movement in each sentence.

1 The monkey leapt through/onto the garage.
2 She carefully put the keys into/onto her bag and closed it.
3 The express train went onto/through a long tunnel.
4 They walked to/along the school as there was no bus.
5 They walked through/along the river until they came to the bridge.

  C

Write sentences about the position of your school, houses and other places in your locality. Use prepositional phrases, such as those listed below, at the end of your sentences.

Example: My friend Hans lives in a house with a red door at the end of my street.

▶ in the pouring rain.
▶ at the end of the street.
▶ over the top of the hill.

Let's make an animated film

In 2011 'The Adventures of Tintin: The Secret of the Unicorn' was adapted and made into an animated film. This is how animated films are made.

Words and sound

5 First, writers brainstorm ideas. The script won't be exactly the same as the book. Next all the actors meet in one room to read their parts aloud to see if the story works. Then the script is revised to make it better. After this the actors record their parts in a soundproof recording studio. The film soundtrack is
10 finally edited down to about 90 minutes in length. The soundtrack is recorded before anything else is done.

Visuals

Next a storyboard made up of many drawings is made for each action in the film. There are thousands of storyboards for
15 a long film. Underneath each drawing are the characters' lines and some instructions for the camera operator and the animator. Then reference drawings are made for each character to show their exact size so that all the artists draw the same way. This way, the film will be smooth, not jerky. Next
20 every frame is drawn on acetate, a clear plastic. Then the drawings on acetate are laid over the background and photographed to make the characters move. Finally the animated film is edited. Characters usually wear the same clothes so that they can be used again and again. The sound is
25 added last.

Word Cloud

brainstorm
edited
script
storyboard

Glossary

acetate a transparent drawing and writing sheet of plastic

animated brought to life, as are the drawings in an animated film

computer generated created by computer software

motion capture computer software that records the movements of people and things

reflective sending back light or heat

soundproof made so that no sound can get in or out

soundtrack the recorded sound, including speech and music, in a film

Filming 'The Adventures of Tintin'

Tintin's film was different. The pictures were computer generated, using motion capture. When a film is made this way, a 3-D computer model is made of the character. It looks
30 like a body. There is an actor for each character who wears a special motion capture suit with reflective markers on it. A computer looks at the way the actor moves and arranges the drawings so that they move like the real actor. The real actor's voice is used in the film. So Tintin looks like Tintin but walks
35 and talks like the actor who is playing him. The computer drawings are matched to the movements of the real actor.

Comprehension

Learning objective
Read and evaluate non-fiction texts for purpose, style, clarity and organization.

A

1 Decide on the six key words or phrases from each paragraph and compare with a partner. Are they the same?
2 The writer is explaining a complex process that happens in a certain order. Find six words and phrases which the writer has used to show the order in which the film is made.

B

Compare the picture of Tintin from the film on this page with the pictures of Tintin on page 52. How are they different and why?

C

If you created an animated film what would it be about?

Discussion time
Reading books and comics, watching movies and playing computer games is interesting and fun. If you were only allowed to do one – either read books or watch movies – which would you choose? Explain your opinion.

Word building

Learning objective

Identify word roots and derivations to support spelling and vocabulary.

Many words are derived from Greek or Latin. There are many groups of words with the same roots.

Example:

Root: know

Derivatives: **know**ledge, **know**ingly, ac**know**ledge

A

Organize the words below into four groups so that words with the same derivation are in the same group.

pain childless reaction act actor painstaking react children take child taken overtake action childlike acting childish painkiller mistake

B

Add a third word to each pair of related words. Use a dictionary.

- **pack:** package
- **obey:** obedience
- **give:** forgive
- **obey:** disobey
- **prison:** imprison
- **joy:** enjoyment

C

List each of the words below under the correct root word.

impress   publicity   discover   impression

relatively   discovery   relative   examination

publication   relation   examiner   relationship

press	public	examine	relate	cover

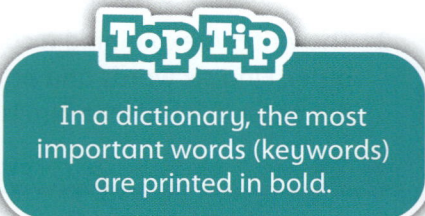

Top Tip

In a dictionary, the most important words (keywords) are printed in bold.

Adverbial phrases

Learning objective
Extend understanding of the use of adverbs.

An adverbial phrase, like a single adverb, gives information about the verb.

Using an adverb:	Using an adverbial phrase:
▶ I will do it **soon**.	▶ I will do it **quite soon**.
▶ She ate her lunch **quickly**.	▶ She ate her lunch **really quickly**.

 A

Add one of the adverbs of degree below to each sentence to make an adverbial phrase.

**quite   really   totally   rather
very   surprisingly   extremely   terribly**

Example: My dad cooks **really** badly.

1 My dad cooks badly.
2 The goalkeeper played brilliantly.
3 My grandpa always drives slowly.
4 She explained the situation clearly.
5 She finished the 5,000 metres fast.

B

Rewrite the following sentences, using the correct adverbial phrase instead of the adverb printed in bold.

Example: He looked at me **strangely**. → He looked at me **in a strange way**.

1 He came to see me **yesterday**.	**A** with great patience
2 My student looked at me **worriedly**.	**B** all over the place
3 She completed the task **carefully**.	**C** with a worried look on his face
4 They waited **patiently**.	**D** the day before
5 His clothes were **everywhere**.	**E** to the top floor
6 I am going **upstairs**.	**F** with great care

 C

Make up four sentences of your own, using each of these adverbial phrases.

quite brilliantly   quite quickly

rather well   extremely carelessly

Remember that 'quite' can have one of two meanings when it qualifies an adverb:

'quite tired' = fairly tired

'quite exhausted' = totally exhausted

Poetry

Learning objective
Read poems by significant poets and compare style, forms and themes.

Word Cloud
angle
busses (US spelling)
flutter
shuttered

Shel Silverstein was an American cartoonist. He was also a poet, a songwriter, a musician and a writer. He died in 1999.

Light in the attic

There's a light on in the attic.
Though the house is dark and shuttered,
I can see a flickerin' flutter,
And I know what it's about.
5 There's a light on in the attic.
I can see it from the outside,
And I know you're on the inside... lookin' out.

Shel Silverstein

New world

Upside-down trees swingin' free,

Busses float and buildings dangle:

Now and then it's nice to see

The world – from a different angle.

Shel Silverstein

Comprehension

A

Explain your answers using evidence from the poems.

1 What kind of atmosphere does each poem have?
   a Terrifying
   b Funny
   c Spooky

2 Find one line in each poem which shows the atmosphere of the poem.

3 Choose what you think is the most important line/lines in each of the poems and compare with a partner.

B

Poet's use of language

1 Where is the narrator (the person talking) in the first poem?

2 Where is the other person in the first poem?

3 Alliteration is when two words close together make the same sound (e.g. grumpy growl). Find two words with alliteration in the first poem.

4 Look at the words 'flickerin' and 'swingin'. What letter in each does the apostrophe replace? Why would the poet choose to write them in this way?

C

1 Three things are odd in the second poem. What are they?

2 Which line rhymes with line 1 in the second poem? Which line rhymes with line 2?

3 Make up a four line poem which rhymes in the same way and draw a cartoon for each line.

Drama

Learning objective
Convey ideas about characters in drama through deliberate choice of speech, gesture and movement.

Here is some dialogue from the comic strips in *The Adventures of Tintin, The Secret of the Unicorn*. Tintin buys Captain Haddock a model of an old ship as a present, which leads to an adventure.

It is written as a film script or 'screenplay'. The initials of the speakers are on the left. The words they say are on the right, but they are not in speech marks (as they are in stories). The stage directions are in brackets. They show what people do and they are always in the present tense.

A

Read the dialogue aloud and listen carefully.

TT I say Snowy, isn't that a fine ship! I've a good mind to buy it for Captain Haddock.

(There is a thundering knock on door.)

CH Are you there, Tintin?

TT Hello, Captain, just the person I wanted to see. I've got a surprise.

CH Tintin, what a magnificent ship! Thundering typhoons! Where did you find this ship?

TT In the Old Street Market. Why?

CH Ten thousand thundering typhoons! What a remarkable coincidence! Imagine! It's remarkable, really remarkable!

TT Is that you in this copy of the portrait?

CH No! It's one of my ancestors, Sir Francis Haddock. Look at the ship in the background.

TT It's the same ship! There's a name here in tiny letters: UNICORN.

(Captain Haddock points to ship.)

CH So there is: UNICORN. I'd never noticed it.

TT Maybe there's a name on mine too... Wait here, I'll go and fetch it.

TT Great snakes! ... It's gone!

B

Read with a partner.

1 With a partner read the dialogue. One of you is Tintin and one of you is Captain Haddock.

2 Do it a second time. This time, look at the punctuation. If you see '!' after a line, remember to emphasize the words. Put expression into your voice.

3 Swap roles and read the dialogue again. Move about this time, acting out your part.

Writing a cartoon

Learning objective
Write new scenes and characters into a story.

Model writing
Look at this four-frame cartoon strip. Alexa and Sabina are strolling along the sea front. Imagine what they say in each speech bubble. Remember that their words do not need to go inside speech marks because they are already in speech bubbles.

Guided writing
Write what each character is saying in the speech bubbles, or number them in your notebook. The first two speech bubbles are done for you, but you can change them if you like.

Your writing
Write and illustrate your own four-frame cartoon strip. You will need to show the following in four pictures.

- the setting (where and when it happened)
- two characters (what they were doing and why)
- a problem (what went wrong)
- what they said (in speech bubbles)
- how they solved the problem (what happened in the end)

Writing a screenplay

 Learning objective
Write a short screenplay.

A **screenplay** is for actors so that they can learn what to say and do in a film before they act it. Stage directions are often adverbs.

Guided writing
Write the cartoon strip on page 64 as a screenplay.

1 Use the layout of the screenplay on page 63 as an example.

2 With a ruler, draw a margin about 3 cm from the left edge of the paper and write the names of the speakers before the margin. Then put a colon (:) after each name.

3 Write what they say on the right of the margin. There is no need to use speech marks.

4 Write stage directions to show what the characters do. Remember to put these in brackets and to use the present tense.

5 The opening is done for you, but you can change it if you like!

(Alexa and Sabina walk lazily along the sea front. Sabina is showing off her new sunglasses.)

Sabina: Mmm! I love ice cream!

Alexa: *(nervously)* Those seagulls look hungry!

Your writing
Turn your own strip cartoon into a screenplay.

1 Look back at the cartoon strip you wrote on page 64. Write it as a screenplay just as you wrote a screenplay for the story of Alexa and Sabina.

2 Read your draft in your head. Check your spelling and punctuation.

3 Ask your partner to take one part. Practise reading your draft. If it doesn't sound real, change it.

4 Do the same with your partner's draft screenplay.

5 Write it out in your best handwriting and practise it so you know exactly what to say and do.

Performance
Perform your screenplays

1 Organize a performance of your scripts for the rest of the class.

2 Choose the five best scripts. Decide who will be the directors and practise acting them till they are perfect.

3 Find some costumes to dress up in.

4 Perform your screenplays to the rest of the school in an assembly.

5 World change makers

Aung San Suu Kyi

Mahatma Gandhi

Shirin Ebadi

Martin Luther King

Let's Talk

The pictures on this page show famous leaders who changed their own countries.

1   What emotion does the person at the centre of each photograph show?

> "Be the change you want to see in the world."
> Mahatma Gandhi

World leaders

Learning objective
Shape and organize ideas clearly when speaking to aid listener.

A

Match the images of the world leaders on page 66 with their country below.

India   Iran   Myanmar   United States of America

B

1   Talk about what makes a good leader for a country.
2   Create three sentences to describe the things good leaders do.
    Example: Good leaders show honesty and care for their people.
3   Say your sentences aloud to a partner or the class.

C

Read about these four leaders and how they changed the world. Use the Word Cloud meanings to help you.

Word Cloud

activist	human rights
equality	justice
fairness	peace
freedom	oppression
honesty	truth

Aung San Suu Kyi has told the world that the people in Myanmar don't have freedom to choose how to live. She has peacefully challenged the rulers of her country. She has been in prison and was kept like a prisoner in her own home. She keeps on speaking out for the people of Myanmar.

Gandhi was given the name of 'Mahatma', meaning 'great soul'. Gandhi gave India and the world the principles of nonviolence and honesty, which are still remembered and used today. Gandhi was killed because of his beliefs.

In the USA **Martin Luther King** was a leader in the Black American struggle for justice and equal rights. He copied the nonviolent methods of Mahatma Gandhi. He was shot dead by people who did not agree with him.

Shirin Ebadi is a lawyer and activist for the rights of women and children in Iran. In 2003, she was given the special international Nobel Peace Prize. She loves her country and said, "My message for Iranians is for love, friendship, peace and justice."

The young Gandhi

As a child, Gandhi was brought up in a loving family and taught to respect all living things. In this story, as a child, Gandhi (Mohan) goes to market with his mother, Ba. He learns that in his religion cows are holy animals.

Word Cloud

bleary   swarmed
flinched   swat
rickshaws   thronged
saris   tottered
scolded   whisked
sprinting

All Living Things

Mohan sat tall, breathing in the tropical scent blowing off the Arabian Sea nearby and the rich smells of spicy cooking. Men and women thronged the dusty road, their great shirts and flowing saris a shifting rainbow of colour, their chatter a mix of Bengali and Hindi

5 languages. Other rich people in rickshaws whisked past, weaving between the people. Soon the Gandhi family driver was sprinting too...

Suddenly the rickshaw stopped. Mohan tumbled out of his seat onto the road. He stared up at the old cow that had tottered in front

10 of them. She froze in place while traffic swerved around her. "Sorry, so sorry!" the driver was saying to the cow, and, "Sorry, Mrs Gandhi."

"Take your time, dear old one," she called to the cow. "The Lord Vishnu is with you." The animals turned bleary eyes in Mrs Gandhi's direction.

15 Mohan rubbed a scraped elbow. "Ba, you care more about the cow than you do about me!"

Her lips pressed together. "I revere all living things." She pointed

to the cow. "You help her," she said, "for dear Vishnu." Mohan looked at his mother for a moment, then at the cow. Her bony shoulder
20 stood higher than his head and flies swarmed around her eyes. "Help her off the road," Mrs Gandhi prompted.

Mohan took a breath and waved the flies from the old cow's face. Big as she was, the cow flinched. "Easy, old girl," Mohan said. He did not know how to move a cow. He picked up a twig to swat her.

25 "Think *ahimsa*, Mohan," Ba scolded. "The ancient Hindu teaching. *Ahimsa*: Nonviolence in all things."

From *Gandhi: Young Nation Builder* by Kathleen Kudlinski

Mahatma Gandhi as a boy

Comprehension

Learning objective
Comment on a writer's use of language; interpret imagery and techniques.

A

Use words and phrases from the extract to support your answers.

1 Which summary of the extract is correct?

   a Mohan and his mother had a traffic accident at the market.

   b Mohan learned that all creatures are important and should be treated gently.

   c Mohan hit the cow to move it away from the traffic.

Glossary

nonviolence a peaceful way of bringing about change (*ahimsa* is the ancient Hindu teaching of nonviolence)

Vishnu a Hindu god

B

What do you think?

1 Give three phrases the writer uses to describe the scene in lines 1 to 7.

2 What imagery is used to describe the people's clothes?

3 Why is the word 'Suddenly' and a very short sentence used in line 8?

4 How does the writer show that Mohan got hurt and felt cross in lines 15 and 16?

5 Ba is described as having 'lips pressed together' in line 17. This means:

   a She didn't like the smells around her.

   b She was smiling happily.

   c She was upset and was thinking carefully.

C

What about you?

1 Write four sentences to describe what happened from the cow's point of view.

2 Have you ever helped an animal? What did you do?

More prepositions

Learning objective

Identify prepositions and know how to use them.

A **preposition** is a word or phrase which shows the relationship between nouns, pronouns and other words in a sentence.
Examples: on, in, under, with, by, to, of

A preposition can be a phrase. *Examples: ahead of, in front of.*
Examples: We arrived home **at** 10 o' clock

We went **to** the old market.

I went to the football match **instead of** my brother.

Prepositions often show:

Time: at one o'clock; **on** Wednesday   **Position: on** the table

Direction: to the shops,   **Possession: with** ideas

Means of doing something: by car   **Accompaniment: next to** her

Exception: apart from the girl

 A

Find six different prepositions in the extract below.

Mohan sat tall, breathing in the tropical scent blowing off the Arabian Sea nearby and the rich smells of spicy cooking. Men and women thronged the dusty road, their great shirts and flowing saris a shifting rainbow of colour, their chatter a mix of Bengali and Hindi languages. Other rich people in rickshaws whisked past, weaving between the people. Soon the Gandhi family driver was sprinting too.

B

Below you will find some prepositions attached to a noun or noun phrase.

Make up sentences so that each phrase comes in the second half of the sentence.

Example: I woke up **during the night**.

1 during the night   **3** by the sea

2 behind the house   **4** since the weekend

 C

Make sentences using the four prepositional phrases in exercise B. Put each phrase at the beginning of a sentence. Insert a comma after the phrase to chunk it off.

Example: During the night**,** I heard a strange sound.

Complex sentences

Learning objective
Begin to use the comma to separate clauses within sentences and clarify meaning in complex sentences.

Complex sentences link ideas together using a **main clause** – a clause that makes sense on its own, and a **subordinate clause**, which doesn't. Look at the main and subordinate clauses in the sentences below.

Main clause	Subordinate clause
She answered her mobile phone	while doing her homework.
She answered her mobile phone	although she didn't want to.

The subordinate clause can be made more important by putting it first. A comma is used to show the separation between the two clauses.

Example: While doing her homework, she answered her mobile phone.

 A

Rewrite these sentences so that the subordinate clause comes first rather than second. Remember to use a comma to separate the two clauses.

1 We will have sweets after dinner if I can find them.
2 There was a knock at the door as he was reading the paper.
3 You should plan your writing before starting to write.
4 The snow fell heavily throughout the afternoon.

Sometimes commas are used to show that additional information has been dropped into the middle of a sentence.

Ellen Singer won the poetry competition. (aged 10)

Ellen Singer, aged 10, won the poetry competition.

Notice the comma on either side.

 B

Rewrite the sentences below to include the information in the brackets. Remember to use two commas – one either side!

1 Mia was late for school yesterday. (my best friend)
2 My father is a good sportsman. (who plays football and swims)
3 Makoto is always falling off his bike. (the boy who lives down the road)

Top Tip
Commas can also be used to 'chunk off' an introductory word or phrase at the start of a sentence. You do this when starting a conversation.
Example: Hello, how are you?

Nelson Mandela

Learning objective
Look for information in non-fiction texts to build on what is already known.

Since the beginning of time, brave men and women have fought for freedom and changed world history.

Early Years

On 18 July 1918, in a small village in South Africa, a great leader was born.

His real name was 'Rolihlahla' which means 'troublemaker' in the language of his tribe. When he went to school, his teacher gave him
5 the name Nelson. Nobody knew what the future held for the little boy and how he would grow up to change the world.

Apartheid

When Nelson was growing up, South Africa was ruled only by white people. They ruled by a system called apartheid, or
10 separateness. This meant that black and white people were separated and could not go on the same bus, to the same shops, schools or hospitals. White people had the best schools, the best hospitals and the best jobs. As a result the black people were poorer and less healthy.

15 ### Working for change

Nelson and his friends wanted to change this. Nelson trained as a lawyer. He organized large peaceful protests against the South African government, which refused to recognize the rights of non–whites. His peaceful protests were
20 met with violence. Many of his friends were killed or imprisoned. In 1964, he was imprisoned too. He stayed in prison for 26 years, refusing to give in to his captors. In 1990 he was released and
25 became the first president of a free South Africa in 1994. He died on 5 December 2013.

Today, South Africa is a democracy, which means that adults choose who they
30 want to run the country. Nelson Mandela made it happen, but it was a hard struggle, and one that had cost him his own freedom.

Word Cloud

captors
government
lawyer
released
separated
struggle
system
violence

Comprehension

 A

Use words and phrases from the extract to support your answers.

1 What did Nelson's real name mean?

2 What did Nelson Mandela have in common with Gandhi? Which two statements are true?

   a Mandela and Gandhi were born in India.

   b They both went to prison for their beliefs and actions.

   c Mandela and Gandhi acted peacefully to protest about lack of freedom.

   d Both men are still alive today.

B

What do you think?

1 Explain in your own words what 'apartheid' means.

2 Most of the paragraphs in the extract have a subheading to help the reader. Think of a different subheading for each of the first three paragraphs and write a new one for the final paragraph.

3 Line 19 says 'peaceful protests were met with violence'. What do you think this means and why was there violence?

 C

In the timeline below there is some missing information. Use the extract to help you complete it.

Nelson Mandela's timeline

> **1918**
> _____

⬇

> **1948**
> The government passes the laws of apartheid.

⬇

> _____
> Nelson Mandela goes to pr_____n.

⬇

> **1993**
> He wins the Nobel Peace prize.

⬇

> _____
> Nelson Mandela becomes the first black _____.

⬇

> **2013**
> Nelson Mandela died on _____.

> "You can use education to change the world."
> Nelson Mandela

Glossary

apartheid a political system in which only some people have full political rights, such as white people in South Africa

democracy a system of government in which all the people can vote to elect their representatives

tribe a group of people who live together and are ruled by a chief

Discussion time

Education is the most important way to change the world, for the better. Prepare a talk to discuss with your class how education can make changes in the world.

Forming plurals

 Learning objective
Investigate spelling patterns for pluralization.

When a word is changed from singular (just one) to plural (more than one) the spelling has to be changed.

Most words add **s**. *Examples*: toy/toy**s**, book/book**s**, table/table**s**.

A

Write the following words out as plurals by adding 's'.

boy   day   meal   girl   car

If the word has a **consonant** before the **y**, **ies** is added. *Example*: ber**r**y, ber**ries**

If the word has a **vowel** (a, e, i, o, u) before the **y**, **s** is added. *Example*: t**o**y - toy**s**

B

Match up these singular and plural words into pairs.

> **baby   days   displays   rays   donkeys   puppy   berry
> delays   city   jelly   berries   boys   toy   key   fly   babies
> cities   jellies   ray   display   monkey   flies   monkeys
> toys   delay   day   donkey   keys   puppies   boy**

The rules of formation of the plural are also used to form the third person singular of the present tense. *Examples*: 'I cry' becomes 'he cries'; 'I play' – 'he plays'; 'I rush' – 'he rushes'

C

1 The words below add **es** when they turn plural. Work out why these words do this. Clue: Say the words aloud, and really pronounce the endings.

Singular	Plurals
box	boxes
dish	dishes
kiss	kisses
lunch	lunches
watch	watches
buzz	buzzes

2 Write out the rule so that it is easy for another classmate to understand.

Plurals and prefixes

Learning objective
Extend earlier work on suffixes and prefixes.

When words end in **f**, or **fe**, and the **e** is silent, the **f** or **fe** is changed to **v** in plurals.

Examples: calf/calv**es**, leaf/leav**es**, thief/thiev**es**, knife/kniv**es**, wife/wiv**es**

A

Find the six errors made in the passage below. Use the examples above to help you, although not all the errors appear in the examples!

Everyone collected things for the picnic in the forest: knifes, loaves – and even some scarfs and gloves in case it got cold! When they arrived, they found the ground covered in leafs. Everyone was enjoying themselfs, eating delicious food and feeding the young calfs who walked by. Suddenly, thiefs jumped down from the cliffs...

Top Tip

When words end in 'ff', or in 've', the plural is formed by simply adding 's'.

Examples: glove/gloves, curve/curves, cliff/cliffs

Prefixes

The prefixes **un–**, **dis–**, **im–**, **in–** at the beginning of a word mean 'not' or 'the opposite of'. They turn a word into its negative.

B

Add the prefix to the words in each column to create negative words. There is no need to change any spellings.

dis–	un–	im–	in–
satisfied	happy	mature	complete
please	popular	possible	correct
harmony	likely	perfect	visible
comfort	dressed	patient	direct
order	professional	polite	accurate

Challenge

Other prefixes which mean 'not' or 'the opposite of' are *il–*, and *ir–*. Use your dictionary to find words which use these prefixes.

C

Prefixes have a whole range of different meanings. Find out what the prefixes below mean and write down their meanings.

Example: The prefix 'sub' means 'below' or 'less than'.

sub–	auto–	trans–	super–	micro–
submarine	automobile	transfer	supermarket	microwave
subhuman	autobiography	transport	superman	microscope
substandard	autograph	transatlantic	superhuman	microchip

Song

Learning objective
Compare style, forms and themes of a poem and a song.

Blowin' In The Wind

How many roads must a man walk down
Before you call him a man?
Yes, 'n' how many seas must a white dove sail
Before she sleeps in the sand?
5 Yes, 'n' how many times must the cannonballs fly
Before they're forever banned?
The answer, my friend, is blowin' in the wind
The answer is blowin' in the wind.

How many years can a mountain exist
10 Before it's washed to the sea?
Yes, 'n' how many years can some people exist
Before they're allowed to be free?
Yes, 'n' how many times can a man turn his head
Pretending he just doesn't see?
15 The answer, my friend, is blowin' in the wind
The answer is blowin' in the wind

How many times must a man look up
Before he can see the sky?
Yes, 'n' how many ears must one man have
20 Before he can hear people cry?
Yes, 'n' how many deaths will it take till he knows
That too many people have died?
The answer, my friend, is blowin' in the wind
The answer is blowin' in the wind

Bob Dylan

Word Cloud
banned
cannonballs
exist
pretend

Hate becomes Love

HATE-HAVE-WAVE-WOVE-DOVE-LOVE

Hate

needed

to have

5 a wave of

friendship

(Hi! How you doing?)

and so it

wove the

10 dove of peace

into

Love

Mike Jubb

Comprehension

A

Explain your answers using words and phrases from the song.

1 The song *Blowin' in the Wind* is about:

 a questioning when the world will change and get better

 b the way the wind blows

 c a man searching for a lost friend

2 Complete the gaps in the sentences below about the song.

 a The white _____ in the first verse is used as an image of peace.

 b The _____ verse is about war and bombs.

 c The songwriter uses two senses, s_____ing and h_____ing, in verse 3.

B

Compare the use of language

1 Find three ways in which the forms of the song and poem are different.

2 In what two ways are the themes the same? Give examples.

C

What about you?

1 Do you prefer the song or the poem? Give a reason why.

2 In what ways can you turn hate into love in your school or community?

Writing a biography

Learning objective
Map out writing to plan structure.

Let's write about a famous person in the past!

Choose your person.

Mary Seacole

Kate and Kamil choose Mary Seacole.

Model writing
Read these notes, then find out more information about Mary Seacole.

1805 Mary Seacole is born. Her father is Scottish. Her mother is Jamaican (had been a slave). Mary's mother heals people with herbs.

1881 Mary dies in London.

1854 The Crimean War begins. Mary works with Florence Nightingale.

1857 Mary writes a book about her adventures.

1853 She goes back to Jamaica. She helps sick people through a yellow fever epidemic.

1851 Goes to Panama. She saves the life of her first patient in Panama.

Writing frame
Draw a timeline and write the sentences from the notebook above in the correct place. Use the past tense.

Write in the dates where you can.

1 Add details in note form. *Example*: mother Jamaican, father Scottish

2 Focus on one event that you would like to highlight. Find out more about that event. Describe it using longer sentences with interesting adjectives.

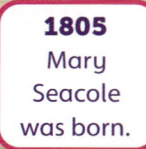
1805 Mary Seacole was born.

1881 Mary Seacole died.

Writing a biographic account

Read the extract on page 72 again. Now write a similar account about Mary Seacole.

Think of a good opening line for your text about Mary Seacole. Write the first draft. Think of ways of making it interesting, such as using unusual adjectives, adverbs and nouns. Encourage your reader to continue reading. Think of a good way to end your text.

Writing descriptions 1

The events in Mary Seacole's life took place in three different countries: Jamaica, England and the Crimea, which is in Russia.

Research

Match photos A, B and C to the countries.

1 Find out more about these different places

2 Where are they?

Vocabulary

Look at the picture of the crowded street in India. Find words and phrases in the extracts to describe the following:

1 The smell in the street

2 The colours of the clothes

3 The speed of the traffic

Writing descriptions 2

Write two sentences describing the street, using the words and phrases you found.

A street in India

6 Sport and health

Round-the-world sailor Laura Dekker on her boat, *Guppy*

American world tennis champions Venus and Serena Williams, when they were young

Sack race at a school sports day

Let's Talk

Look at the three pictures.

1 Would you like to sail round the world like Laura?
2 What are the children doing on sports day?
3 What is your favourite sport? Do you like watching it or doing it?

"You have to believe in yourself when no one else does — that makes you a winner."
Venus Williams

Sports vocabulary

Learning objective
Explore definitions and use new words in context.

Word Cloud

achievement
passion
record
succeed

A

1 Write a sentence about your favourite sport or activity.

2 Explain your choice to a partner and describe how your sport is played.

3 Tell your partner about your best event at school sports day and your worst, and explain why.

> Some young people are very determined to succeed at a sport. Laura Dekker was born on a boat and is the youngest girl to sail round the world by herself.
>
> The Williams sisters were very poor so their father taught them tennis on public courts. They became the best female tennis players in the world.

4 What else did Laura and the Williams sisters need to do to succeed at their sports?

Example: They needed to believe in themselves.

B

Are you a team player?

Do you like playing sport alone, in pairs, or in a team? Make a list of sports you can play alone, in a pair, or in a team.

Examples:

Alone	In pairs	In a team
ice skating	tennis	football

C

1 Copy the sentences below, filling in the correct word from the list.

ambition   record   achievement   passion

My favourite sport is (your sport)_____. It is my _____.
My _____ is to break a _____ one day. That would be a real _____.

2 Write one or two sentences about your dream sporting adventure. It could be on land, water, or in the air. Present and explain your adventure to the class.

Catching the moon

This is a fictional story based on a real person – a young American girl, Marcenia Lyle – who dreamed of becoming a professional baseball player in the 1930s. One day the manager of a famous team came to choose boys to attend a baseball day camp in the summer holidays…

Word Cloud

defence
famous
professional
striking
teasing

The Winning Run

When Mr Street approached the players after the game, Marcenia crowded in close so he could see her.

"I just saw some good ball," Mr Street said, smiling. "Who wants to come to my baseball camp and really learn to play this game?"

5   Every hand went up.

Mr Street shook them all. He shook Marcenia's hand last. "You've got a good arm, little miss, and you run fast," he said. "But I don't take girls in my camp."

Marcenia looked down so no one would see her disappointment.
10   She began striking dust from her dress.

"Marcenia's been playing ball with us since we were little kids," Harold told Mr Street.

"She's the only player we got who ever steals bases," Clarence said.

Marcenia was pleased that her friends had come to her defence,
15   but Mr Street didn't change his mind. As she walked home, she thought about how these very same boys had teased her when she first started playing baseball with them. Then when they saw she could run, hit, and throw as well as they could, the teasing stopped. They had let her play.

Glossary

base in baseball, one of the four positions that a player must reach in order to score points

baseball a game invented in America

home plate the place where the person hitting the ball stands and where they must return to after running around all the bases

steal base (or 'steal home') running to a base or to the home plate before another player from your team hits the ball

20 Marcenia decided to give Mr Street a reason to change his mind.

Every day Marcenia played baseball and every day Mr Street refused to invite her to his camp. Then came a day when Marcenia got tired of hearing him say, "I don't take girls in my camp." That day, when she was on third base in the ninth innings of a tie game,
25 Marcenia decided to take the biggest chance in all baseball...

With the ball speeding toward home, Marcenia dropped her weight and slid into home plate. She had stolen home and scored the winning run.

From *Catching the Moon* by Crystal Hubbard

"I just loved the game, but the guys weren't ready for me. So many of them thought it was a disgrace to play with a girl, but my heart was set – and I kept at it. You gotta keep trying."

Comprehension

Learning objective
Comment on the writer's use of language and explain reasons for his or her choices.

 A

Give evidence from the text in your answers to A and B.

1 How long had Marcenia been playing baseball?

2 Was Marcenia as good as the boys?

3 What did the boys think about Marcenia playing with them at first?

4 Did girls usually play baseball at this time?

B

Writer's use of language

1 Why has the writer used the title *Catching the Moon*? Explain your reasons.

2 Why and how did Marcenia try to change Mr Street's mind?

3 How does the writer show Marcenia's feelings in lines 9 to 10, and 14?

4 Why does the writer repeat the phrase 'every day' in line 21?

 C

What about you?

1 Marcenia decided to take a risk to prove how good she was. What would you have done?

2 With a partner, take the roles of Mr Street and Clarence. In your role, write down three reasons for or against Marcenia joining the camp. Present your arguments to the class.

The real Marcenia achieved her ambition and became a professional baseball player. Then she changed her name to 'Toni Stone'.

Reported speech

 Learning objective
Understand the difference between direct and reported speech.

In **direct speech** the words which are actually spoken go inside speech marks.

Example: **"**She's the only player we've got who ever steals bases,**"** Clarence said.

If it was a comic, the words inside the speech marks would be inside a speech bubble.

Reported speech is when we are reporting or telling what someone has said. It doesn't need speech marks.

Example: The team **told** Mr Street **that** Marcenia was the best player they had.

 A

Decide which of the sentences below are direct or reported speech.

1 The sports coach told his team to get ready.

2 Peter declared, "I like football better than athletics!"

3 Sumara told her friends that she wasn't going to the basketball match.

4 "I really enjoyed the game!" exclaimed the teenager.

5 Salvador whispered that he had forgotten his football kit.

B

Change the direct speech in the sentences below to reported speech. The first one has been done for you. Notice the addition of that, the change of pronoun, and the change to a tense further back in time.

1 "I can finish the painting today," he said.

He said **that he could** finish the painting that day.

2 "I really like swimming!" she declared.

3 "Can I have some salad?" asked the boy.

4 "Are you going to see the new volleyball team, Maria?" asked Fatima.

5 "I hope you all like the meal," said the chef.

C

Too much direct speech in writing can become boring and confusing. Write out the dialogue below, but change the two direct speech sentences in red to reported speech.

"Are you going to come with me tonight to watch the game?" asked Maria.

"No," replied Juliet.

"Why not?" Maria said.

"I would rather watch this good film on television. It's meant to be quite scary," Juliet explained.

"Oh, that's a shame," replied Maria.

She's the only player we got who ever steals bases.

Dialogue and direct speech

Learning objective
Set out dialogue correctly using a range of punctuation.

When writing out direct speech, the reporting clause can come:

▶ at the **start** of the sentence

Example: **She announced**, "I really do like baseball, and I think my team will win!"

▶ in the **middle** of the sentence

Example: "I really do like baseball," **she announced**, "and I think my team will win!"
(Note that there is no capital letter in 'and' as it is not the start of a new sentence.)

▶ at the **end** of the sentence

Example: "I really do like baseball, and I think my team will win!" **she announced**.

 A

Rewrite each sentence, putting the reporting clause in the position shown in red.

1   He exclaimed, "I hope when you play for our team, you will score many goals!" **end**

2   The head teacher announced, "I am glad to say there has been an improvement in behaviour, but not by everyone." **middle**

3   "If you practise hard you will be able to compete in the Olympic games," the coach whispered. **start**

Commas separate the reporting clause from the direct speech.
Example: He asked**,** "Why aren't you coming with me?"

"I think," he said**,** "I might come with you."

 B

Add commas to the direct speech below. Decide whether you need one or two.

1   "I would like to go to the beach this weekend" he said.

2   "I think" she replied "it would be a good idea."

3   "Marcenia is very upset" she whispered.

 C

Write three of your own sentences which use direct speech and include a question or an exclamation mark.

Full stops, question and exclamation marks are usually part of direct speech so put them **inside** the speech marks.

Learning objective
Locate information confidently.

Sailing Solo

Laura Dekker, the youngest sailor to circumnavigate the globe single-handedly, arrived at the Caribbean island of St Maarten on 21st January 2012. She survived weeks at
5 sea with just a few cockroaches for company – and did her homework too.

She said, "I became good friends with my boat. I learned a lot about myself."

She was born to sail

10 Her Dutch parents were living on a yacht in a port in New Zealand when Laura was born, and she was six when she first sailed solo. At eight, she decided her dream was to sail round the world and, aged just 13, Laura sailed solo
15 from the Netherlands to England and back – a trip her father hoped would "cure her wanderlust".

Dangers and discomforts

On her round-the-world trip she took on six
20 metre high waves and extreme weather – on one occasion, heading to the Cape of Good Hope in Africa, her storm jib (a sail used in storms) got jammed. She finally managed to take it down in the early hours of the morning.
25 Another of her sails ripped completely during

Laura alone at sea on *Guppy*

the voyage. She slept on a damp bed and lived on rice and pasta, with cookies and pancakes an occasional treat. She dodged near collisions with cargo ships and worried about pirates.
30 Not in the least squeamish, she had to rescue live flying fish that had flung themselves into her cabin. She survived weeks at sea with no company – except for the rats and cockroaches that had stowed away in her cabin. On top of
35 all that, she had to do schoolwork.

Adapted from *The Guardian* January 2012

Glossary

circumnavigate to go round the world

globe world

solo by yourself

Word Cloud

cargo
cockroaches
dodged
extreme
jammed
squeamish
yacht

Comprehension

Learning objective
Develop note-taking to extract key points of the text.

A

Give evidence from the text in your answers to A and B.

1 What age was Laura when she first sailed solo?
2 Describe what happened to Laura near the Cape of Good Hope.
3 What dangers did Laura face, apart from the sea?
4 Write a summary sentence for each of the three paragraphs, giving the key fact.

B

What do you think?

1 Compare the photographs of Laura on pages 80 and 86. How does she look? How do you think she is feeling in each one?
2 Write a different title for the article and suggest different subheadings.

C

What about you?

1 What sporting success has your country, city or school achieved?

Discussion time
"It is okay for a person under 18 to travel alone at sea for such a long time." Do you agree or disagree? Give your reasons.

The Optimist is a small sailing dinghy for children up to the age of fifteen. Laura sailed hers solo when she was six. They are simple, safe, and have only one sail. Children sail them in competitions.

2 How would you try to persuade adults to let you do something new and difficult, such as sail a dinghy on your own?

Complex and simple sentences

 Learning objective
Identify unfamiliar words, explore definitions and use new words in context.

The story of Laura Dekker uses long and complex sentences as well as difficult vocabulary. This makes it hard for younger children to read and understand.

A

Look at the non-fiction text again and compare it to this simpler version.

Laura Dekker is a young sailor. A sailor is a person who sails on boats in the sea, but sometimes it can be on rivers. Laura is the youngest person in the world to sail around the world on her own. Her trip ended on an island. This island is called St Maartens. It is in the Caribbean Ɗ which is near America.

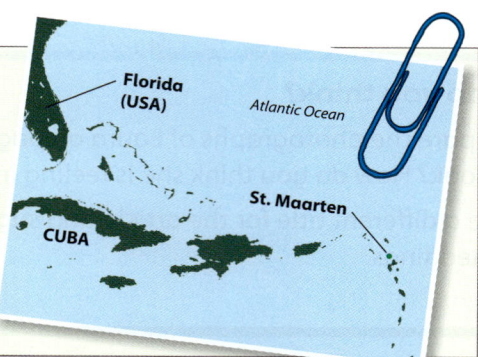

Notice how:

1 Sentences are shorter.
2 Vocabulary is simpler.
3 New terms are explained.
4 More information is given.

B

Choose one of the following sentences, and write it out again so that it is simple for younger children.

▶ At eight, she decided her dream was to sail around the world and by thirteen she had accomplished her plan.

▶ On one occasion she took on six metre high waves while enduring extreme weather conditions.

C

The Word Cloud on page 86 lists words whose meaning you might know. It helps to learn a word if you explain it to someone else.

1 Choose three words from the Word Cloud and write definitions for younger children.

2 Choose six other words from the non-fiction text and write easy to understand definitions for each one.

Commas in complex sentences

Learning objective
Use the comma to separate clauses within sentences and clarify meaning in complex sentences.

Commas can be used to separate off information about a person.

Example: Laura Dekker, the youngest person to circumnavigate the globe, arrived at the Caribbean island of St Maarten.

Top Tip

When using commas to separate off information about a person, you could underline or write the information in a different colour. This would help you to remember the commas.

A

Insert two commas in each of the following sentences, so that information about the person is separated off. The first one has been done for you.

1 Maria, who is 25 years old, won the competition.
2 Mrs Brownlea the new principal is very popular.
3 Dan filled with despair slumped to the ground.
4 Lucian 15 years old decided today was his happiest day.
5 Johannes an elderly person fell off his bicycle last night.

B

Form sentences using the information below. Remember to insert a pair of commas to separate off information after the name.

1 Janita 85 years old was the oldest person to run the London marathon.
2 Fatima Khan resident of Bangalore has achieved the impossible in her race.
3 Andres the fastest cyclist in the world has won another gold medal.
4 Ahmed 10 years old with a missing front tooth ran into the classroom.

C

Rewrite the sentences from B but this time use brackets to separate off the extra information. What difference does this make?

Fun run

Learning objective
Read poems by significant poets.

People run marathons (a road race) either because they are athletes and are trying to break a time record or because they want to raise money for charity. Their friends might sponsor them. *Example*: by giving a certain amount per kilometre. If you finish the run, you can raise a lot of money. This poem describes a fun marathon.

Glossary

armour a metal suit to protect you from danger

croquet a game played on grass where you hit a ball through hoops

lasso a rope with a sliding noose at the end, used for catching cattle

liner a passenger ship

Loch Ness monster an ancient creature which is supposed to live at the bottom of a lake in Scotland

toga a piece of cloth worn by Roman men

The Marathon

I'm going to run the marathon,
wearing a diving suit,
strapped to a parachute.
With a cloak and staff like Noah,
5 pushing a garden mower.
In a ballet dancer's tutu,
cracking a cowboy's lasso.
Yes, I'm going to run the marathon,
inside a suit of armour,
10 leading a Tibetan llama.
As an ancient prince from Khartoum,
in a Loch Ness Monster costume.
As a camel from Tangier,
or an astronaut in space gear.
15 *Yes, I'm going to run the marathon,*
As a green and grotty ogre,
in an Imperial Roman toga.
As a bridegroom on his wedding day,
or someone dressed to play croquet.
20 In a dragon costume from China,
as a luxury ocean liner.
Yes, I'm going to run the marathon
and I want to get myself seen.
Although maybe, just maybe,
25 I think it might be best
to forget all these wacky ideas
and stick with shorts and vest!

Brian Moses

A

1 Read the poem.

2 Look at the pictures and the words in the glossary. Talk about the words which you do not recognize.

3 What sentence is repeated in this poem?

4 Look at the first seven lines. Which pairs of words rhyme?

5 Which pairs of words rhyme in lines 9 to 14?

A sporty poem

Learning objective

Ask questions to develop ideas and extend understanding.

A

Read as a class split into two groups. Listen to the rhythm of the poem *The Marathon* and clap.

1 Group 1, read all the lines in red.

2 Group 2, read all the lines in black.

3 Read it aloud again with Group 1 reading the lines in red and Group 2 reading the lines in black. Clap to the rhythm.

B

Copy the box below and make pairs of words which rhyme.
Example: a polar bear, a monster with blue hair,

1 Complete the poem with a friend,

2 Now read out your poems. One of you says, "I'm going to run the marathon," while the other reads the lines that rhyme.

> **My Marathon Poem**
>
> I'm going to run the marathon,
>
> dressed as a polar bear,
>
> or a monster with blue hair.
>
> _____
>
> _____
>
> _____
>
> _____

A marathon in fancy-dress is a challenge.

Word Cloud

marathon
sponsor

Runners taking part in a marathon

Let's Talk

If you wanted to raise money, what would it be for? Would it be for your school sports club? Would it be to help sick children? What else could it be for?

How much would you ask for every kilometre you run?

Keeping a diary

Learning objective

Explore the features of texts which are about events and experiences. *Example*: diaries.

Laura kept a diary every day when she sailed round the world. She sent it to her family and friends. They wanted to know that she was safe. She might have written like this.

Monday, 6 December

I'm in the harbour at Cape Town today. Dad and his friends helped me to buy all my food and water for the next part of the trip. We packed everything carefully so that it can't get wet. I checked my list to make sure that I hadn't forgotten anything. I'm excited about leaving tomorrow morning.

Tuesday, 7 December

I didn't sleep well because I was so nervous. This morning I was pleased because the sea was calm. Lots of people came to wave goodbye and some boats sailed beside me for the first few kilometres to keep me company. Then I was all alone again.

Wednesday, 8 December

The wind is perfect and I'm sitting here writing this in the sun. Lots of dolphins came and played around the boat and kept me company. I'm getting used to being by myself again. I tried to do some schoolwork this afternoon but dolphin watching is more fun. They aren't scary like the whales I saw last month.

Thursday, 9 December

It began to get really rough and the waves crashed and the boat rolled along. It's still very rough. But the strong wind is good as we are going the right way. I've been wearing my waterproof clothes and staying in the cabin for hours to keep dry. I saw the cockroaches again. They have become my friends and I don't mind them.

Friday, 10 December

It wasn't quite so rough today and the flying fish kept jumping into the boat. I don't like it when they smash on the deck or fall into the cabin. They smell if I don't get rid of them quickly. Please try to send me a message tonight. I've sailed 150 kilometres since Tuesday. Give Spot a hug and a bone for me. It would be so nice to have him on board, but dogs can't come on a journey like this.

Model writing

Read the diary carefully.

1 What do you notice about most of the verbs in the diary.

2 What pronoun does Laura use when she is writing about herself?

3 Does she write as if she's talking to a teacher or as if she is talking to friends?

 Learning objective
Use pronouns, making clear to what or to whom they refer.

Top Tips

You need first person pronouns to write a diary

e.g. 'I', 'we', 'us', 'my', 'our'

Be informal; write as if you are talking to friends.

Writing a diary

Look at the map which shows where Laura went. Choose a place to start from. Pretend that you are Laura and write your diary for seven days. You can make up anything you like.

▶ You could discover a mysterious island.

▶ A whale might almost overturn your boat.

▶ You could be shipwrecked on an island.

▶ You might have seen a mermaid.

▶ You could have rescued some sailors.

▶ An albatross might decide to take a free ride on your boat.

Writing frame

Use the writing frame as a guide.

My Diary

Day 1	
Day 2	
Day 3	
Day 4	
Day 5	
Day 6	
Day 7	

Revise and check ❷

Vocabulary

1 Complete the sentences with adverbs made from the list.

excited kind anxious furious

  a The parents were worried and waited _____ for their children to arrive.

  b It was his birthday and he ran _____ towards the post box.

  c He slammed the door _____ and ran out into the yard.

  d She felt sorry for the child and spoke to her _____.

2 Write out these words and underline the prefix. Explain what each prefix means. Give examples of five more words, one for each prefix.

  a microscope

  b autograph

  c submarine

  d transfer

  e supermarket

Punctuation

1 Rewrite the sentence twice so that the reporting clause – 'she announced' – comes in a different place each time. Remember to punctuate correctly!

she announced I have always loved reading ever since I was given my first Tintin book when I was six.

Grammar

1 **Write the sentences in direct speech and punctuate correctly.**

   a Scott told us that it was a brilliant match.

   b He announced that he was going to start training too.

   c He said he wanted to be part of the winning team.

   d He hoped we would all support him and asked us to wish him luck.

2 **Write the sentences in reported speech and punctuate correctly.**

   a "Tell me how you came to be here, Captain," Tintin asked.

   b "Well," said the Captain, "someone rang up from the hospital."

   c "Go on," said Tintin, "tell me what happened next."

   d "You are not going to believe me!" said the Captain.

3 **Rewrite each sentence adding a prepositional phrase from the list.**

on Saturday night   behind the station   in the mountains
by train

   a The family decided to take a holiday _____.

   b They travelled together _____.

   c They arrived late _____.

   d They found the hotel _____.

Spelling

1 **Write the plurals of these words:**

   a lunch   **d** puppy *

   b knife   **e** donkey

   c buzz   **f** toy *

   Explain the spelling rule for the words marked with *.

2 **Rewrite the sentences putting the words in bold into the negative.**

   a The **happy** girl was **mature** for her age.

   b It was very **professional** of the player to be so **polite**.

   c The fans were **pleased** with the result.

7 Making the news

Let's Talk

1 Look at the images and list all the different ways of receiving the news.

   Example: podcast of radio news on an MP3 player

2 How does your family get the news?

3 What kinds of news articles are you interested in?

   Examples: sport/music/film and TV stars/world events

> "If you don't like the news, go out and make some of your own."
>
> Wes Nisker

Who makes the news?

Learning objective
Identify unfamiliar words, explore definitions and use new words in context.

Word Cloud

c _ _ _ _ _ _ a
inte _ _ _ _ _ w
_ _ _ _ _ op
m _ _ _ _ o _ _ _ _ e

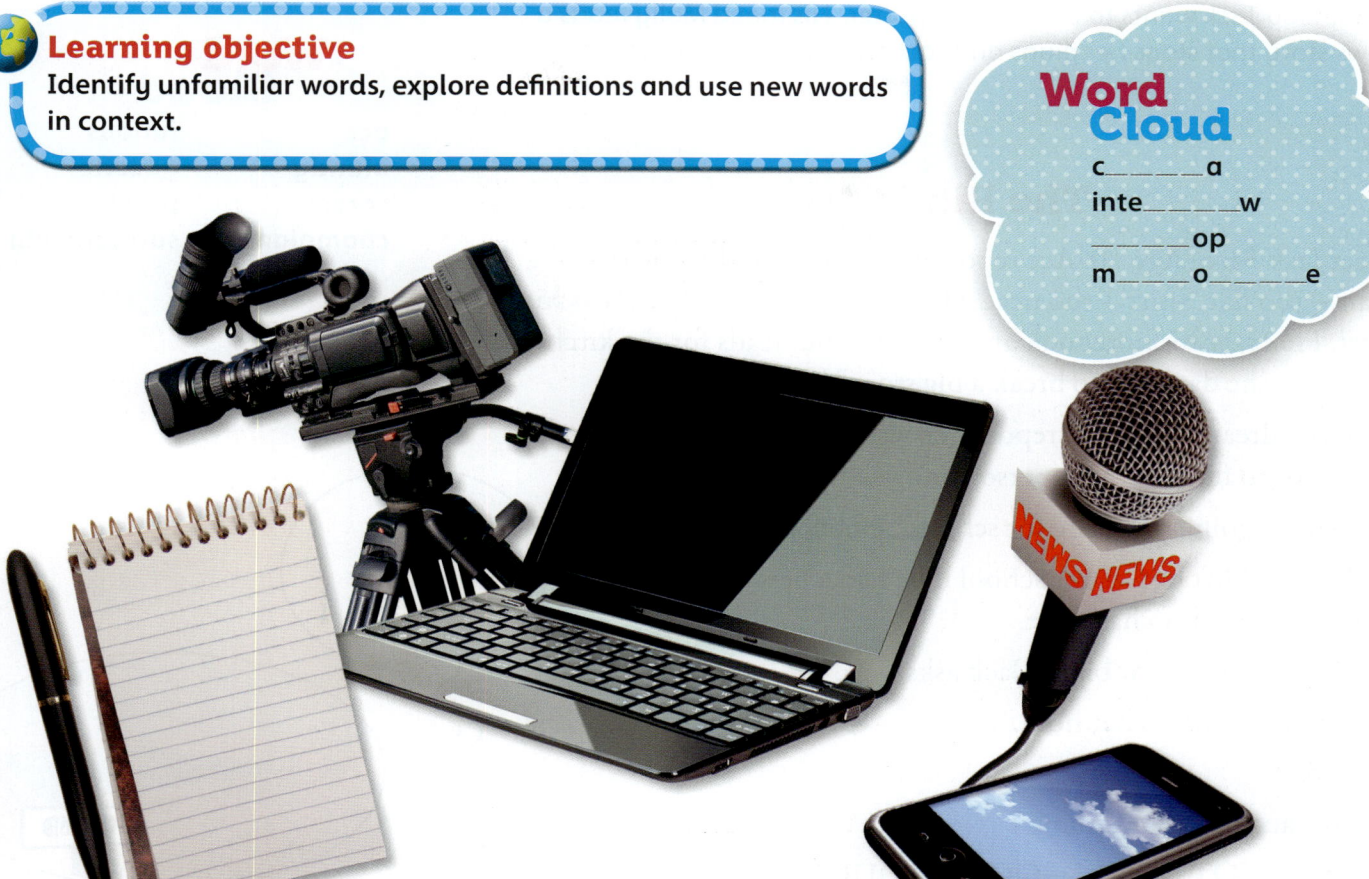

A

Use the pictures to help you fill in the Word Cloud with things and actions a journalist needs to create or report a news story. Then add more words.

B

1 Use some of the words below to complete the sentences about how to write a good news article.

quotation   headlines   reporters   photographers   articles correspondents   editor   news   podcast

a To add more interest to a news article use a _____ from the people involved in the event.

b _____ are short phrases at the beginning which tell the reader about the topic of the article and try to catch attention.

c _____ take pictures with a digital camera or smartphone.

d Reporters in charge of a specific topic or area of the world are called _____.

2 Write a sentence definition for the words above you haven't used.

Jack Rico – reporter

Schoolboy Jack wants to be a news reporter. His friend Molly reads a news story that stops her plans and Jack tries to interview her.

Word Cloud

ace
bluntly
career
championship

furious
gazette
plonks
sarcastically

The Big Story

Meet Jack Rico. Age 10. Ace reporter. He looks in the mirror. Hair – too flat. Shirt – too neat. He spikes his hair and untucks his shirt. He grabs his notebook and his pens and heads for the kitchen. "Today is the day I get to break a big story," he tells himself.

5   Jack's dream is to get a report he's written in *The Norton Gazette*. He needs to find the right person and ask the right questions.

"You're going to be late for school," shouts his mum.

He wouldn't be late for school if he had a new bike, but his mum won't let him have one.

10   "Can I have a new bike?" Jack asks.

His mum shakes her head.

"Why?"

"Because," says his mum.

"BOY NOT GIVEN GOOD ENOUGH ANSWER BY
15 MOTHER," says Jack, who sometimes talks in headlines.

Later at school...

Jack is sitting next to Molly, his best friend. She doesn't look too happy. "BEST FRIEND IN SAD FACE SHOCK," comments Jack. "What's up?" Molly plonks a copy of *The*
20 *Norton Gazette* on to the desk.

The headline screams: ***Deadly bug shuts pool.***

Terrified lifeguards rushed to shut down Norton Swimming Pool yesterday after routine tests on water samples showed signs of Cryptosporidiosis which can cause
25 *illness or even death. The pool was shut immediately.*

"Great story," says Jack.

"Glad you're seeing the good side," says Molly sarcastically.

"What's the matter?"

"The pool is where I train. There isn't another one for miles. It's
30 the Under-11s championship swim competition in two weeks. If the pool stays shut, I've got no chance of winning."

"A follow-up story," says Jack, reaching for his notebook.

"GIRL'S SWIMMING CAREER DESTROYED BY DEADLY BUG. I'll write it and take it to the *Gazette* after school. I knew this

35 would be the day I'd finally get a story printed."

"I'm glad losing my chance in the championship makes you so happy."

"I'm not happy about it," says Jack. "But it's the news. I've got to report it. Just answer a few questions."

40 "How does it feel to have your swimming career ruined before it's even begun?" Jack asks bluntly.

Molly gives Jack a furious look.

"I'm not answering that," she snaps. "Report something that can get the pool re-opened if you want to be any help."

From *Project X: The Big Story* by Dominic Barker and John Bradley

Glossary

break a big story write and publish an important news report

Cryptosporidiosis a common waterborne disease caused by a parasite

Comprehension

 Learning objective
Consider how the writer expresses point of view and how the characters are presented.

A

Give evidence from the text in your answers to A and B.

1 Why does Jack spike his hair and untuck his shirt before going to school?

2 What does Jack want his mum to buy for him?

3 Is Molly actually happy with Jack's response to the news story?

4 Why is Molly upset with the newspaper report about the pool?

B

Writer's use of language

1 Why has the writer used 'headlines' speech for Jack and what effect does it have?

2 What words are used to present Molly?

3 How do the words about Molly create her character and express her emotions?

C

What about you?

1 Think of an eventful day at school and write three 'headlines' from that day.

2 Read your headlines to a partner. Can they guess what your event or story is about?

Opposites

Learning objective
Investigate ways of creating opposites. *Example*: un–, im– using comparatives and superlatives.

A

In the extract 'The Big Story', the prefix **un–** is used in the word 'unpack' to mean the opposite of packing.

1 Create new words by adding **un–**.

able believable acceptable attached aware certain breakable comfortable clean convinced fasten lucky noticed real safe wanted reasonable truthful well

2 Use six of these words that are new to you in sentences.

B

The prefixes **dis–, in–, il–, ir–** and **im–** also mean 'not'.

Examples: **dis**appoint, **in**justice, **il**legal, **ir**regular, **im**polite.

1 Attach the right prefix to the root words below. Be careful, as it is easy to get them mixed up. It would be wise to check in a dictionary first!

___ possible ___ believe ___ legible ___ rational ___ visible

2 Find two more words beginning with each of these prefixes.

C

We can make comparisons using adjectives.

To compare two things or people, use the **comparative** form with **–er** or 'more...'. *Example*: shorter, more famous

To compare three or more things or people, use the **superlative** form with **–est** or 'most...'. *Examples*: smallest, most expensive; important, more important, most important

Fill in the missing gaps in the table below.

old		oldest
	hotter	
new		
		funniest
beautiful		
		most careful
	thinner	
	sillier	
pleasant		

Tricky Spellings

Is it a two-syllable word ending in **y**? Drop the **y** and add **–ier** or **–iest**.
Example: happy/happier/happiest

Is it a one-syllable word ending in a single consonant? Double the consonant before you add **–er** and **–est**.
Example: wet/wetter/wettest

Sounds the same – but different spelling

Learning objective
Revise grammatical homophones.

Homophones are words that sound the same but are spelt differently and have a different meaning. They are a common cause of spelling mistakes.

A

they're, their and **there** are three words that sound the same.

Here is a way to remember their different meanings:

- If it means 'they are', write **they're**.
- If it means 'belonging to them', write **their**.
- If it means something else, write **there**.

Fill in the gaps in the following sentences.

1 I put my book over _____.

2 The children found _____ missing coats.

3 I looked in the cloakroom but my coat wasn't _____.

4 They picked up _____ new shoes.

5 _____ not coming tomorrow, I don't know why.

6 _____ is no doubt that _____ singing is what _____ famous for.

B

where, we're and **wear** are three words with different meanings.

Here is a way to remember how they are different:

- If it refers to a place, write **where**.
- If it means 'we are', write **we're**.
- If it is to do with clothes, write **wear**.

Fill in the gaps in the following sentences.

1 _____ going to the shops tomorrow.

2 What are you going to _____ to the party?

3 _____ have you put the book?

4 _____ are you going? _____ going to see _____ the shops are, and what we can buy to _____ .

Challenge
Think of ways to remember the difference between 'who's' and 'whose', and 'it's' and 'its'.

A newspaper for you

FirstNews | **FirstNews TV** | **SUBSCRIPTIONS**

First News is a weekly newspaper aimed at 7–14 year olds. It is in tabloid format, and aims to present current events alongside news on entertainment, sport and computer games. It is published on Fridays and is read by over one million children every week all

5 over the world. The newspaper was launched in May 2006.

Bursting with content!

Every issue is packed from cover to cover with the latest stories about world and home affairs, the environment, sports, entertainment and puzzles, all selected to engage and inspire

10 its readers.

Meet two of the *First News* team

The *First News* team includes editors, writers, designers and many more.

Rich is the Design Manager, which means that he has to make the

15 paper look good and add all the pictures. That isn't always an easy job.

Ben is the Website and Marketing Assistant. Ben is a big fan of all things entertainment – film, TV, magazines – you name it, Ben's got something to say about it. An interesting fact about Ben is

20 that he is really tall. He loves writing, hanging out with friends and visiting different places.

Word Cloud

editors
launched
newspaper
published

Get *First News* delivered every Friday!

First News is the ONLY weekly newspaper for young people. It is now the widest-read children's publication with over 1 million readers every week!

First News journalists provide up-to-date, insightful and dynamic articles on a range of subjects from entertainment to politics, sport to science which will be really interesting to students aged 7–14.

Treat a special child in your life to a *First News* subscription and they will discover a read which is vibrantly presented, thought-provoking, intelligent – and fun! Don't miss out – subscribe NOW.

Comprehension

Learning objective
Compare writing that informs and persuades.

Glossary

current events news about things happening now

home affairs events that happen in or close to the country in which the newspaper is based

marketing assistant a person who helps to tell people about a product or service

tabloid format square pages

 A

True or false?

1 *First News* is a monthly paper for adults.

2 Each issue always has a sports section.

3 The very first issue was published last Friday.

4 There over 100,000 readers each week.

 B

What do you think?

1 Which is the best description of the text on the website?

   a It contains only facts.

   b It contains mostly facts.

   c It contains mostly opinions.

   d It contains half facts and half opinions.

2 The information in both extracts is about the newspaper *First News* but the style of language is different. One is a news feature report and one is a persuasive advert.

   Find two phrases in each text to show how they are different.

C

What about you?

1 What job would you like to have on a newspaper?

2 Which features of a newspaper do you think are the most interesting?

Discussion time
Good news stories should contain only true facts and not opinions. Do you agree or disagree? Explain your opinion to a partner.

Idioms

Learning objective
Investigate the origin and appropriate use of idiomatic phrases.

Idioms are common sayings. Their meaning is figurative – so the meaning is different from what the words mean. The idiom used in the *First News* extract, 'hanging out with friends' means Ben likes to see his friends, not actually 'hang' with them.

A

Many idioms would be absurd if the words were true and taken at face value. From the list below, choose two idioms you find particularly absurd and draw what the words literally say.

1 He visits us only once in a blue moon. (rarely)
2 They fought tooth and nail to win the fight. (fought very hard)
3 The young man had a chip on his shoulder. (angry today about something that happened in the past)
4 The spelling test was a piece of cake. (a task that was completed very easily)
5 The new coat cost an arm and a leg. (was very expensive)
6 The child's behaviour was driving me up the wall. (was annoying me very much)

B

1 Many idioms use pairs of words. Choose the correct missing words to finish the phrases.

graces   square   dogs   neck   riches

a The two horses were running neck and _____.
b We won the competition fair and _____.
c She has gone from rags to _____ almost overnight.
d The weather was terrible; it was literally raining cats and _____.
e Ever since she has won the talent show, she has given herself airs and _____.

2 Match the meanings below to the idioms above.

fairly, with no cheating   go from being poor to rich
very heavy rain   think one is better than everyone else
exactly even

Fixed idioms:
If an idiom contains two different nouns, you cannot change the order of the nouns.

Suffixes

Learning objectives

Use effective strategies for learning new spellings.

Use known spellings to work out the spelling of related words.

The word endings **–tion**, **–cian**, **–ssion** are all pronounced as in sta**tion**.

The word ending **–sion** is pronounced as in sta**tion**, or as in deci**sion**.

A

The ending **–cian** is used in the names of many jobs. Match the jobs with the definitions.

Example: A musician plays a musical instrument.

beautician   electrician   magician   mathematician
optician   politician   laboratory technician

1 A/An _____ examines your eyes.

2 A/An _____ does strange tricks that look impossible.

3 A/An _____ takes care of your skin and hands.

4 A/An _____ fits and repairs electrical things.

5 A/An _____ works in the government.

6 A/An _____ studies numbers and shapes.

7 A/An _____ works with machines and instruments.

B

You can change a verb ending in **–de** or **–se** into a noun which ends in **–sion** (pronounced as in deci**sion**).

Examples: divide → division; revise → revision

Complete the sentences by changing pairs of verbs into nouns.

Example: To avoid possible confusion, I'm making some revisions to this term's maths exam.

explode / collide   decide / divide   exclude / include
revise / confuse   conclude / provide

a The football fans were surprised by the _____ of Lazzio in the team, and the _____ of Bari from it.

b Immediately after the _____ of a truck with an oil tanker on the highway, there was a huge _____ .

c The government's _____ is to make _____ for a disaster fund.

d The family had to make a _____ about the _____ of the farm among the farmer's brothers.

List poem

This poem shows how we use words all the time in different ways and for different reasons.

Words Are Ours

In the beginning was the word
and the word is ours:
the names of places,
the names of flowers,
5 the names of names,
words are ours.
Page-turners
for early-learners
How to boil an egg
10 or mend a leg
Words are ours
Wall-charts
Love hearts
Sports reports
15 Short retorts
Jam-jar labels
Timetables
Words are ours
Following the instructions
20 for furniture constructions
Ancient mythologies
Online anthologies
Who she wrote for
Who to vote for
25 Joke collections
Results of elections
Words are ours
The tale's got you gripped

Have you learned your script?
30 The method of an Experiment
Ingredients for merriment
W8n 4ur txt
Re: whts nxt
Print media
35 Wikipedia
Words are ours
Sub-titles on TV
Details on your cv
Book of great speeches
40 *Guide to the best beaches*
Looking for chapters
on velociraptors
Words are ours
The mystery of history
45 The history of mystery
The views of news
The news of views
Words to explain
the words for pain.
50 doing geography
Autobiography
What to do in pay-phones
Goodbyes on gravestones
Words are ours.

Michael Rosen

Learning objective
Read poems and comment on style, forms and themes.

Comprehension

 A

Match each phrase below with a line from the poem printed in italics.
The first has been done for you.

1 The 400 metres race was won by Maria Flores.   *Sports reports*
2 The beach is cleaned every morning.
3 IN LOVING MEMORY OF HENRY DAVIS
4 Strawberry Jam, Hilltop Farm
5 A daffodil is a spring flower.
6 Pain: the feeling in your body when you are hurt
7 Place the egg in a pan of boiling water.

 B

What do you think?

Look at the poem and find examples of:

▸ some things which are found in schools
   Example: 'Wall-charts'
▸ some things which aren't found in schools
   Example: 'What to do in pay-phones'

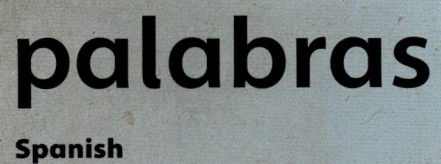

palabras
Spanish

C

What about you?

What subject or book topic in each pair sounds the most interesting to
you? Give reasons for your answers.

1 the mystery of history, or the history of mystery?
2 a book of great speeches, or a guide to the best beaches?
3 the views of news, or the news of views?

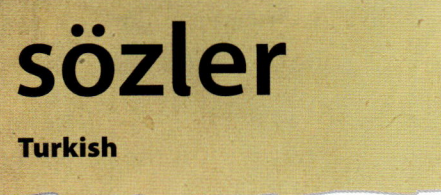

sözler
Turkish

Arabic

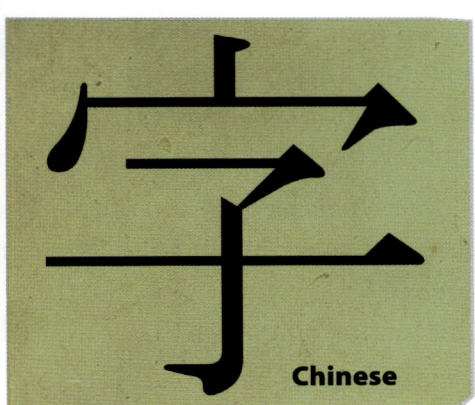

Chinese

Hindi

A newspaper article

> **Learning objective**
> Organize and write a narrative news story, including direct speech.

Look at the picture from a news story. What do you think happened?

Model writing

Match the six steps for organizing a story with the paragraphs in the article below (a–f).

1 Write a headline that sums up the story. Grab the reader's attention with emotive words or alliteration.

2 Clarify the meaning of the headline. Introduce the topic with facts and figures.

3 Involve the reader. A good way to do this is through a dramatic or emotional quotation.

4 Develop the story.

5 Describe people's responses with a quotation.

6 Conclude the story in a strong memorable way. Use emphatic adjectives and idioms.

FINALLY, make your story more interesting by adding an illustration, a photo, a map or a graph. **Remember**: A picture is worth 1,000 words.

a) More chickens mean poor families have more birds to sell, raising money to buy food, or pay school fees. "We seem to have struck lucky with this idea!" say the advisers, who have now helped more than 3,700 families.

b) "We need to take drastic action. We can't go on like this!" said one desperate farmer.

c) "At first I thought it was a joke, but the chicks move about freely within the compound while the hawk is up in the trees, and he has never taken any since I tried it," says one farmer.

d) The farmers were visited by an adviser from the UK and were told to try a new and creative method. They dyed the birds pink and purple with a common antiseptic called Gentian Violet. The hawks took no notice of the brightly coloured birds!

e) Farmers in Tanzania are dyeing their chickens pink and purple to stop hungry hawks from eating them. Chickens are worth about $5 each and in Tanzania some farmers earn no more than $10 a month. One farmer lost 36 chickens in a month – that is more than he earns in a year!

f) Farmers in Tanzania paint chickens pink and purple!

Article by Jan Walter

In your notebook, write down the verbs used in the story opposite in the correct order on the lines below. Do not include verbs from quotations.

▶ **Past tenses**: lost, _____

▶ **Present tenses**: paint, are dyeing, _____

▶ **Present perfect**: have helped, _____

Writing a newspaper article

Write a similar story about farmers protecting their animals. Follow the six steps given on page 108. Use these notes that a journalist made in Namibia, Africa.

1 drop in cattle deaths

2 farmers keeping guard dogs in Namibia – stop cheetahs eating their animals.

   last year, 1 farmer lost 12 sheep + 10 goats

3 "need to act to protect our animals"

4 adviser: keep guard dogs with the herds 24 hours a day. Cheetahs afraid of big guard dogs.

5 "Cheetahs don't come near our cattle; they go off and hunt deer instead." "We don't have to kill cheetahs (endangered species)" Number of cheetahs in Namibia – stopped falling

6 "Good idea!" "Very happy!" 200 working dogs in guard dog programme. Farmers get help with dog care and training.

Revising your story

Notice how the writer on the opposite page used different words to avoid repeating the same one. *Example*: bird, chicken, chick, hawk

Use different words in your story (see examples below).

Now revise your story to add a variety of vocabulary.

Examples:
cattle / cows / livestock
cheetahs / big cats / predators
dogs / guard dogs / hounds / Anatolian shepherds (a type of guard dog)

8 Flying high

Let's Talk

1 The four pictures are of different flight inventions. Choose the one you know least about and think of two questions you'd like to find the answers to.

2 Why do you think flying is so important to human beings?

> "For once you have tasted flight, you will walk the earth with your eyes turned skywards."
>
> Leonardo da Vinci

Flight inventions

Learning objectives

Ask questions to develop ideas and extend understanding.
Shape and organize ideas clearly when speaking to aid listener.

Word Cloud

advance   invention
booster   ornithopter
experiment   scientific
exploration   shuttle
flight   technical
ideas

A

Match the captions to the pictures on page 110.

1   A model of Leonardo da Vinci's ornithopter – flying machine
2   The space shuttle is launched by two rocket boosters
3   A birdman flies in his super lightweight wingsuit
4   The Boeing Dreamliner is so light it uses less fuel than a normal aircraft

B

Read the notes below and prepare to give a short talk to the class about the ornithopter.

1   Leonardo Da Vinci was born in Vinci, Italy, 1452.
2   Became a famous artist and inventor.
3   Fascinated by how birds flew.
4   Wanted to invent a machine to help human beings fly like birds.
5   Designed the ORNITHOPTER – which flapped its wings like a bird.
6   But only a drawing – never actually built and tested.
7   Recently, Todd Reichart built an ornithopter based on Da Vinci's drawing and tried flying it. It flew 145 metres in 19.3 seconds at a speed of 25.6 kilometres an hour.
8   Today people still try and fly like a bird using special fabric wingsuits.

C

How have aeroplanes and air travel made a difference to the world? Think of two positive and two negative points. Use words from the Word Cloud to help you explain.

The first successful flight of a powered aeroplane was by the Wright brothers in 1903.

Flying adventure story

 Learning objective
Comment on a writer's use of language and explain reasons for the writer's choice.

Word Cloud
cascaded   ploughed
flicked   scramble
flinching   swerve
grasping   tumbled
hurtled

Sam, Zara, Marcia and Ben are involved with the secret invention of a flying boat but a mysterious organization wants to steal their discovery. They are sitting in the plane when suddenly…

The Silver Turtle Takes Off

"Armed police!"

"Armed police! Stand still!"

Before the children could think what they should do, an elderly woman wearing a battered suede jacket came careering round the side of the hangar on a bicycle. "Help
5 me inta* the plane!" she gasped, leaping from her bike and letting it fall onto the pebbles by the slipway. She flung herself at the *Silver Turtle*, her hands grasping the edges of the open cockpit canopy, her feet struggling to find the step-holes in the plane's side. Bewildered, but fearing the old woman might fall backwards, the children held her arms and helped her scramble in. She tumbled down into the pilot's seat, shot
10 out a bony hand, and released the brake lever.

"*No*!" shouted Zara, as the *Silver Turtle* rolled forward. Marcia and Ben both made a grab for the brake lever but, with surprising strength, the woman pushed them back and flicked two switches labelled PORT MOTOR and STARBOARD MOTOR. The propellers whirred into life and the plane hurtled down the slipway towards the sea.

15 "What are you *doing*?" yelled Ben. He'd got himself back into the co-pilot's seat. Should he pull the woman away from the controls? No – going too fast. They'd swerve off the slipway and crash onto the pebbles.

Sam clung to the sides of the nose hatch, alarmed and
20 powerless, watching the sea come nearer and nearer…

SPLASH! The plane ploughed into the water and a plume of sea spray cascaded down over the open cockpit and hatch. Without flinching, the woman revved the motors to full speed and zoomed the plane onward through the sea. Keeping one hand on her
25 control column, she punched the undercarriage button and the three wheels whirred and clunked up into the hull.

"STOP!" shouted Zara, sprawled across the back seats with Marcia.

"Stop?" cried the woman. "Are you *mad*?"

30 PTANG! Something had ricocheted off the plane, just behind the cockpit. Zara looked back through their tail spray and saw two armed men shooting at them from the increasingly distant shore.

The woman was starting to pull back her control column. "NO!" shouted Sam, realizing what she was doing.

35 The spray vanished, the sea fell away beneath them and they soared up into the sky. The *Silver Turtle* was airborne.

From *The Flight of the Silver Turtle* by John Fardell

* Scottish people sometimes say "int**a**", meaning "int**o**".

Glossary

careering moving with great speed around a corner or bend

cockpit the place in an aircraft where the pilot sits

column gear stick

hangar a large covered space to store an aeroplane

port the left-hand side of a ship or aircraft when you face forward

ricocheted bounced off something

starboard the right-hand side of a ship or plane when you face forward

Comprehension

Explain your answers using words and phrases from the text.

1 Read the statements about the story. Which two are true?

a The four children are on the plane.

b Ben stops the elderly woman.

c Armed police fire at the plane.

d The plane stays on the sea.

2 Why did the writer use these types of verbs? Choose **one** correct answer below.

a They make the story more interesting.

b They help you to imagine you are there.

c They suggest lots of quick action and movement.

3 Choose two verbs you think are really powerful and explain why.

Writer's use of language

1 Read the paragraph starting at line 21 and find **six** past participles that end in **–ed**.

Example: cascaded

What about you?

What would you have done if you had been Sam?

Getting the verb tense right

Learning objective
Understand conventions of standard English, the agreement of verbs.

 A

A student has written a suspense story. You will see that he has used many good techniques, but has got many of the verb tenses wrong! These are in bold, coloured blue. Rewrite the extract below, correcting the verbs.

> Slowly, very slowly, Ali **approach** the old, wooden door. What **were** on the other side? Fumbling, he **insert** the key in the lock, the thick darkness of the night **make** it difficult. Eventually, it **click**. He **make** the first turn. A second. A third. Bit by bit, it **were** turning, turning, turning, the noise echoing through the cold night air. What would he **be finding** on the other side? He **were** scared. Very scared indeed.

 B

Write these sentences out fully, putting the verbs in the correct tense.

1 I was sorry that I had _____ the vase, because I _____ it. (smash/like)

2 While the nurse _____ him, she _____ some tea. (examine/make)

3 He _____ very slowly all the way home, as the clutch had _____ (drive/break)

4 The gardener _____ his lunch, then _____ the vegetable patch. (eat/dig)

C

Make up four sentences using each of the verbs below in two different tense forms. This means you will have eight sentences in total.

Example: I tried to catch the ball. He caught the ball. (to catch)

1 to draw

2 to forget

3 to speak

4 to lose

Synonyms

Learning objective
Collect synonyms and investigate shades of meaning.

Synonyms are words which have nearly the same meaning as another word or expression – but not quite. 'Horrible', 'nasty' and 'disgusting' are synonyms for 'bad' – but mean very different things. It is important to use the right synonym in your writing so that the meaning is clear for the reader.

The verbs 'went', 'eat' and 'said' are known as weak synonyms, as they do not tell the reader precisely how something was done.

A

Look at the difference between the verbs in these sentences.

Juan went across the classroom.	→	Juan strolled/dashed/crept across the classroom.
My cousin ate a mango.	→	My cousin nibbled/munched/gobbled a mango.
"I hate flying," he said.	→	"I hate flying," he yelled/whispered/muttered.

1 Choose a synonym to replace the blue word in the sentences.

tumbled   grasping   shouted   rolled   scrambled

Marcia and Ben **sat** down into the pilot's seat.

"Stop!" **said** Zara as the plane **moved** forward.

Holding the edges of the door, she **got** into the plane.

2 A new girl, Anna, arrives in the classroom. In the writing below, the verb synonyms used show her to be shy and quiet. Change these so that Anna becomes bold and confident.

Anna **crept** into the classroom. "Where do I sit, Sir?" she **muttered**.

"Over there, Anna," replied the teacher, pointing at an empty chair.

Anna **shuffled** across the room. "I hope this is the right chair," she **whispered**.

Discover hot air balloons

Glossary

altimeter an instrument used in aircrafts for showing the height above sea level

balloon's envelope the fabric part of the balloon that fills with hot air

cockerel a male chicken

GPS Global positioning system which uses satellites to find the position of a vehicle or a person

nylon a very strong man-made material

scan reading to find specific information

skim reading reading quickly to get a general idea of the subject. The subheadings help with this

It's all hot air

The first hot air balloon passengers were a sheep, a duck and a cockerel! In 1783 they travelled for seven minutes in a balloon built by Frenchmen Joseph and Étienne Montgolfier. Later that year the two men flew across Paris.

5 How hot air balloons work

Hot air is lighter than cool air, so a balloon rises when the air inside it is heated. Modern hot air balloons have gas burners which heat the air inside the balloon's envelope. The gas in the four tanks in the basket makes a 'whoosh' sound as it travels up the hoses and into the burner. 10 A balloon will go higher or lower depending on how much gas is burned.

Flying hot air balloons

Some people have balloons for fun while others enter competitions in them. Large pleasure balloons carry passengers who pay for the 15 flight. It is even possible to fly over the Egyptian pyramids in a balloon. While the balloon is up, somebody follows it with a car and trailer, ready to collect the people and equipment on landing. They are in touch with the crew by radio.

Balloon pilots navigate with a map, 20 which is often on a laptop. They also have a GPS, so that they know where they are. An altimeter tells them how high they are.

How modern hot air 25 balloons are made

The balloon's envelope is made of very strong nylon. The bottom part of the envelope is made of 'Nomex', a fabric which cannot catch fire. Steel cables attach the basket and burners 30 to the balloon's envelope. The cables go under the basket, so it is very strong.

envelope

skirt

parachute valve cord

burners

wicker basket

propane tanks (inside)

Balloons are sometimes used for advertising.

Comprehension

> ### Learning objective
> Read and evaluate an explanation text for purpose, style, clarity and organization.

A

Give evidence from the text to support your answers.

1 What travelled for seven minutes in 1783?

2 What makes a hot air balloon go higher?

3 In a hot air balloon, how is the air inside the balloon's envelope heated?

4 Why can't hot balloons catch fire?

5 Compare your answers with a partner's.

B

What do you think?

1 What is the purpose of *It's all hot air*? Which two statements are correct?

   a To explain how hot air balloons work

   b To persuade the reader to go on a hot air balloon trip

   c To inform the reader about hot air balloons

   d To argue that hot air balloons are important

2 What is the purpose of the subheadings?

3 Choose one paragraph that you think is very clear. 'Convert' it into a drawing to explain the topic clearly to someone else. Don't forget to label parts of your drawing.

C

What about you?

Plan and write a step-by-step route for a hot air balloon trip. The route will be above your town, city or province and be of interest to those flying in the balloon. The car and trailer have to follow the balloon's route on the ground.

Example: START: take off on the school sports field

First place of visual interest is the botanic gardens and wildlife park…

Word Cloud

burners	hoses
cables	navigate
fabric	trailer
envelope	

What did this pilot forget to do? Why did the balloon not go up? OOPS!

Discussion time

"Aeroplanes pollute the atmosphere and this damages our environment. People should travel less by plane for business and holidays." Explain why you agree or disagree.

Words ending in –*ed* and –*ing*

Learning objectives
Know the rules for the spelling of words ending in –ed and –ing.
Know rules for doubling consonants.
Learn spelling rules for words ending in –y.

Most core words simply have **–ed** or **–ing** added to the end.
Examples: yell yell**ed** yell**ing**; gasp gasp**ed** gasp**ing**
If the original word ends in an **e**, this **e** will be dropped when you add **–ing**.
Example: live liv**ed** liv**ing**

A

1 Add **–ed** and **–ing** to the words below. Write two more words which fit
the rule. *Example:* name nam**ing** nam**ed**
live bake love save dance

If the original word ends in a consonant, and has a short vowel sound before it, then the
consonant is doubled when you add **–ing** or **–ed**. *Example*: drag, dragged, dragging

2 Copy out the grid below and fill in the gaps.

drag	dragged	dragging
drop		
grab		grabbing
shop	shopped	
stop		
whir		whirring
skim	skimmed	

B

Look at what happens when a word ending in **–y** changes to an ending with **–ed** or
–ing.

carry	carried	carrying
marry	married	marrying
cry	cried	crying
try	tried	trying

Write a grammar rule for what happens when a word ends in –*y*.

Remember new spellings

 Learning objective
Use effective strategies for learning new spellings and misspelt words.

Here are some of the new words you have learnt in this unit.

**suede   ricochet   basket   balloon   material   envelope
navigate   fabric   whirred   technical   plough**

A

1   Read, say and listen to the words.
2   Put the words in alphabetical order.
3   Give a definition for each word.

Here are some tips.

> **Write the word out and make the difficult letters large or different.**
> sUEDe
> fabriC
>
> **Break the word into syllables or chunks.**
> bask-et
> mat-er-i-al
> tech-ni-cal
> ric-o-chet
>
> **Find a word inside the word.**
> There is a **ball** in **balloon**
> There is a **gate** in **navigate**
>
> **Check for a spelling rule.**
> **Whir** ends in a consonant *r*, and has a short vowel sound before it, so double the consonant when *-ed* is added.
> whir → whirred

B

Look at your definitions from A to help you write a sentence using each new word.
Example: I usually sit next to my mum while she is driving so I can read the map and navigate.

The freedom of flight

 Learning objective
Read poems by significant poets and begin to interpret imagery and techniques, e.g. metaphor.

Word Cloud

blasting	scorching
cruising	shooting
flame	space-man
mission	swifter

Soft Landings

Space-man, space-man,
Blasting off the ground
With a wake of flame behind you
Swifter than passing sound.

5 Space-man, ace-man,
Shooting through the air,
Twice around the moon and back
Simply because it's there.

Space-man, place-man,
10 Cruising through the skies
To plant your flags on landscapes
Unknown to human eyes.

Space-man—race, man,
Scorching back to earth—
15 To home and friends and everything
That gives your mission worth.

Howard Sergeant

Comprehension

A

Give evidence from the poem to support your answers.

1 Who is waiting for the space-man at the end of his mission?

2 Find at least four 'space' words and think of more.

3 Match each verse with a summary word from the list and think of one more.

Return   Flight   Launch

Verse 1 _____

Verse 2 _____

Verse 3 _____

Verse 4 _____

••••Challenge••••

Sport is often used as a metaphor for life.

Example: My **goal** is to get a grade A in English. (goal/football)

Think of three more examples.

B

Poet's use of language

1 What words does the poet use to describe the space flight?

2 Which prepositional phrase in each verse shows the progress of his journey?

3 Which verbs give a sense of speed and movement?

4 The first line of each verse is nearly the same. This is because…

    a it gives the poem rhythm and repetition.

    b the rhyme sounds good.

    c the poet couldn't think of anything else.

C

What about you?

1 Do you like the poem? Explain why or why not.

2 Would you like to visit space? Explain why.

Writing a suspense story

Learning objective
Choose words and phrases carefully to convey feeling and atmosphere.

The Flight of the Silver Turtle was a very effective suspense story because it made the reader want to keep reading to find out what would happen next.

Writers use techniques to make their stories exciting for readers.
Example: Instead of only describing what is happening a writer uses conversation between characters to move the story along clearly.

Model writing

1 Read the extract below. The coloured notes at the side explain which techniques the writer has used to create suspense.

Action and movement are part of the dialogue so that readers can imagine the action.

Use of adverbs.

The use of strong, precise verbs suggests things **happening**.

Bad weather and darkness are included to create an atmosphere.

Notice where the commas have been placed!

"Oh, I'm so bored," moaned Mohamed, throwing himself down on the bed. "Nothing ever exciting happens round here."

"Yeah," Jon agreed, flopping back wearily in the chair opposite him. "I don't want to spend the whole summer break hanging around, getting bored."

They both sat for a minute in silence, staring morosely at the rain battering against the window. It was only 7 o'clock, but already the sky was dark and forbidding.

Suddenly, Mohamed jumped up. "I know, let's go and explore the old cafe on the main road. I've heard the door has been left open. What about it?"

"Yes, yes!" Jon shouted excitedly. "Why not? Let's get going!"

2 Read part two of the story and find examples of more techniques used in suspense writing. Copy the table below and write in your examples.

The use of strong, precise verbs that suggest things happening.

A sentence that begins with a present participle verb.

Use of adverbs.

Use of commas to mark off phrases and clauses

Use of simile

What is this punctuation device called?

As they approached the old cafe, they began to feel scared. Very scared indeed. Why on earth had they come here? The night was pitch black, the road was deserted. Moaning eerily, the wind whipped angrily around their ankles, like a fierce dog.

5   Jon shuddered. "Perhaps we should go back. It looks like—"
"No," Mohamed interrupted, not wanting to show him that he was scared too. "Just a quick look, and then we'll go home. It won't take a minute."
What was left of the old cafe was now in full view. Run down,
10   dirty, neglected, its windows broken and torn blinds flapping in the cold night wind. Clouds covered the moon. A sudden bang came from behind them. They both shivered. Nervously, very nervously, they both crept towards the open front door...

Technique	Example from part 2
Strong, precise verbs	
Sentence starting with present participle verb	
Adverbs	
Commas to mark off clauses	
Simile	
Punctuation device	

Your writing
Write your own beginning to a suspense story.

Part 1 Begin with two friends who are bored and decide to go and investigate something.

Part 2 Have them moving towards the place, but stopping just before they open the door. Use the techniques listed below in your writing.

- Dialogue to move the plot along
- Some movement and gesture built into the dialogue so that the reader can SEE what is going on
- Strong verbs, and adverbs
- Some short sentences

- Rhetorical questions
- Similes
- Repetition
- Commas (in the right places!)
- Extreme weather and darkness
- Sudden noise

9 Tales and legends

"There have been great societies that did not use the wheel, but there have been no societies that did not tell stories."

Ursula K. LeGuin

Let's Talk

1 These pictures show how traditional stories are passed around from one person to another. What is happening in each picture?

2 What two questions would you ask the characters in each picture?

124

Traditonal tales and legends

 Learning objective
Read and identify common features of tales and legends.

A

Match the words with their definitions.

fable   legend   loyalty   quest   trickster   values

Example: an ancient story which has been passed down through the ages = legend

> an ancient story which has been passed down through the ages

> a person who lies to cheat other people

> the important things in life that people believe in and act upon

> a special search involving a journey

> a story which has a moral lesson to teach

> faithfulness to a friend or a family member

Typical features of traditional tales and legends

Characters: talking animals or fantasy creatures, wizards, queens, princesses, kings and princes, rich and poor, good and evil, wise and foolish

Actions: courage and determination, kindness, helpfulness, patience

Settings: a long journey, happened long ago, dangerous places, palaces, mountains, lakes

Themes: a gift or an object with special and unusual powers, a quest to find a person or an object, a reward or a penalty

Narrative structure: repetition, sequential organization, patterns in the plot, crisis and solution, 'happy ever after' endings

Aesop is believed to be a storyteller from ancient Greece, but we don't know whether he really existed.

A tale from China

Learning objective
Explore the text features of traditional tales and legends.

Word Cloud

bellowed   squawking
flocks   swung
jiffy   throne

Tchang, a young boy from China, is on his way to visit the Great Wizard of the West. He needs to ask him why he and his mother are so poor. On his journey Tchang meets three others who help him on his way and who also have questions for the Wizard. The Pearl Dragon is one of the three friends.

Tchang and the Pearl Dragon

Tchang was about to run away, but the dragon called to him. "Don't be frightened! I'm quite harmless. Tell me why you want to cross my river."

Tchang explained that he needed to ask the Great Wizard of the
5 West some important questions.

When the Pearl Dragon heard the questions, it smiled. "You're a good lad, Tchang," it said. "Hop on my back and I'll have you across in a jiffy."

On the far side of the river, Tchang thanked the dragon.

10 "Think nothing of it!" the dragon replied cheerfully. "That's what I'm here for. Oh, by the way. While you're there, could you please ask the Wizard why I can't fly? Every dragon in China can fly – except me." Naturally, Tchang said yes. He set off again towards the West with the four questions going around and around in his head.

15 Forty-nine days later, he came to the golden palace of the Great Wizard of the West. The palace was carved out of a mountain. It took Tchang a whole day to climb the million steps up to the huge door. When he pulled on the bell rope, the mountain shook. Flocks of eagles rose squawking into the air from a thousand golden towers.

20 The great doors of the palace swung open. Tchang found himself in a mighty hall. It was so high he couldn't see the ceiling for clouds. On a throne at the end of the hall sat the Great Wizard. He glared down at Tchang. "Well?" he bellowed. "What do you want, boy?"

Tchang tried to stop shaking. "I … I have four questions to ask
25 you, sir!"

"HAH!" shouted the Wizard. "Then you may as well go home right now! I will only answer THREE questions. If you ask me four, I won't answer any of them. So there!"

Tchang thought his legs would fold underneath him. What
30 could he do? There was his poor mother's question, then the old
woman's question, then the old man's question, and then the Pearl
Dragon's question. For his own sake, as well as his mother's, he
desperately wanted to know the answer to the first question – but
he also knew he couldn't let his friends down. So he answered sadly,
35 "Then I will only ask you three."

From *Dragon Tales* by Andy Blackford

Glossary

by the way an expression used as an aside, an extra

for his own sake! for himself

in a jiffy! very quickly

So there! an expression of firmness

Think nothing of it! don't worry about it

Comprehension

 Learning objective
Provide accurate textual reference from more than one point in a story to support answers to questions.

 A

Put the parts of the extract in the correct order.

1 It took Tchang a day to climb up the million steps to the door of the Wizard's palace.
2 Tchang was afraid to ask the Wizard his questions.
3 The Pearl Dragon told Tchang to ask the Wizard why he couldn't fly.
4 Tchang hopped on the dragon's back in order to cross the river.

 B

What do you think? Give evidence from the extract to support your answers.

1 How was Tchang feeling when he first spoke to the Wizard?
2 Find three different words that show that the Wizard is angry.
3 Find two features of traditional tales and legends that the writer used in Tchang's story.

 C

What about you?

1 Tchang had to choose three of the four questions to ask the Wizard. Which three would you choose and why? All the questions are in the story on pages 154–160.
2 Write the next part of this traditional story. Choose either **a** or **b** below as your starting point.
   a The dragon persuades Tchang to go back in to see the Wizard and try again. **OR**
   b Tchang travels home with only three answers and meets his questioning friends on the way.

Discussion time
Writers of traditional tales and legends use a 'story' to teach a moral lesson. Read the full story of Tchang on pages 154–160. What do you think is the 'lesson' within the story?

Pronouns

 Learning objective
Use pronouns, making clear to what or whom they refer.

Pronouns are used to replace nouns so that we do not keep repeating them.
The writing below does not use any pronouns, so it is difficult to understand.

Jack asked Henry's mother if Jack could play with Henry and May. Henry's mother replied that Henry and May had just gone out with Ashok, Usha and Fatima, and that Henry, May, Ashok, Usha and Fatima had all gone to the park. Jack was very disappointed. Jack really wanted to play with Henry, May, Ashok, Usha and Fatima.

A

Fill in the missing pronouns.

them   he   they   she   he

Jack asked Henry's mother if _____ could play with Henry and May. _____ replied that _____ had just gone out with Ashok, Usha and Fatima, and that _____ had all gone to the park. Jack was very disappointed. _____ really wanted to play with _____ .

There are different types of pronouns.

Personal pronouns	These replace a noun or pronoun in a sentence.	I, you, me, him, she, he, her, they, we, them, us, it
Possessive pronouns	These replace a noun in a sentence and also show ownership.	theirs, mine, yours, his, hers, its, ours

 B

Choose four personal pronouns and four possessive pronouns and write eight sentences, using each one correctly.

 C

Which group of pronouns do 'myself', 'themselves', 'ourselves' belong to?

Commas

 Learning objective
Use commas to separate clauses within sentences and clarify meaning in complex sentences.

Commas are used in different ways within a sentence:
- ◗ To separate a main clause from a subordinate clause
- ◗ To separate off words and phrases

A

The examples below from *Tchang and the Pearl Dragon* show you the different ways commas are used. Add two examples of your own for each category. You might want to copy the examples and just change some of the words.

When to use a comma	Examples from *Tchang and the Pearl Dragon*
To separate a main clause from a subordinate clause	◗ When the Pearl Dragon heard the questions, it smiled.
Before 'but'	◗ Tchang was about to run away, but the dragon called to him.
After a prepositional phrase or an adverbial phrase	◗ On the far side of the river, Tchang thanked the dragon. ◗ Forty-nine days later, he came to the golden palace of the Great Wizard of the West.
After a small 'tag' word	◗ "Oh, by the way." ◗ Naturally, Tchang said yes.
Before directly addressing someone	◗ "You're a good lad, Tchang." ◗ "What do you want, boy?"
A list of phrases	◗ There was his poor mother's question, then the old woman's question, then the old man's question.

B

Make up six sentences, each of which use commas in one of the ways listed above. Then remove the commas – or put them in the wrong place – and ask a friend to correct the sentences. Did they get them right?

C

Make up a table like the one used in A. Fill in examples of the different uses of the comma from newspapers, books and magazines.

Instructions for making a plate

Learning objective
Read and evaluate an instructional text for purpose, style, clarity and organization.

People love to be told stories. Even pieces of art and kitchen plates can 'tell' stories through their images. The willow pattern plates were first painted over 200 years ago. Each image on the different sections of the plate tells a different part of the story of two people who fell in love.

A willow pattern plate

How to make and paint a willow pattern plate

What you need:

- Clay
- Sheet of plain paper
- Rolling pin
- Two pieces of wood 40 cm long, 4 mm thick
- Plate-sized circular object
- A plastic card
- Piece of soft leather
- Paints for painting on ceramics
- Someone to fire your plate
- Someone to help you cut the clay

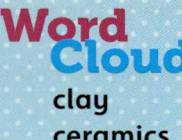

Word Cloud

clay
ceramics
potter

Follow steps 1 to 11 carefully

1 First, roll out the clay between the two pieces of wood.

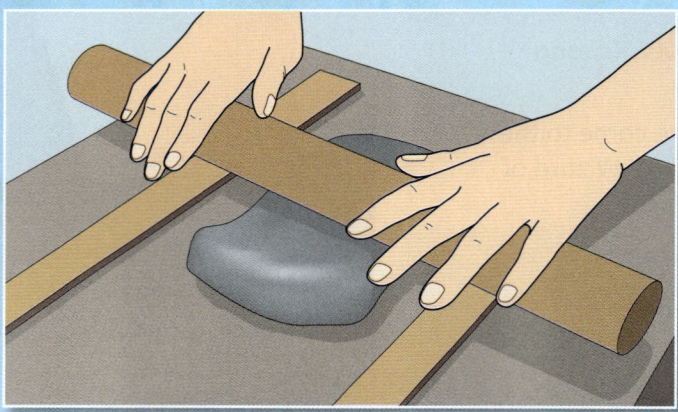

2 Turn the clay and roll again, and again.

3 Then place the clay on paper and smooth it out with a plastic card.

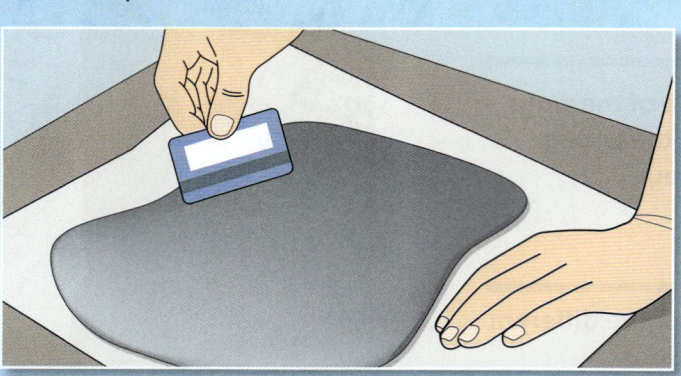

4 Repeat this on the other side.

5 Next, place a circular object on the clay and cut around it.

6 Cut slits in the leftover clay to help remove it.

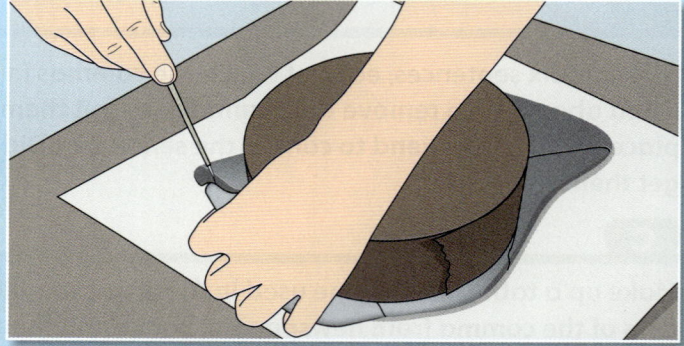

7 Make the leftover clay into thin 'rolls' to build support pieces.

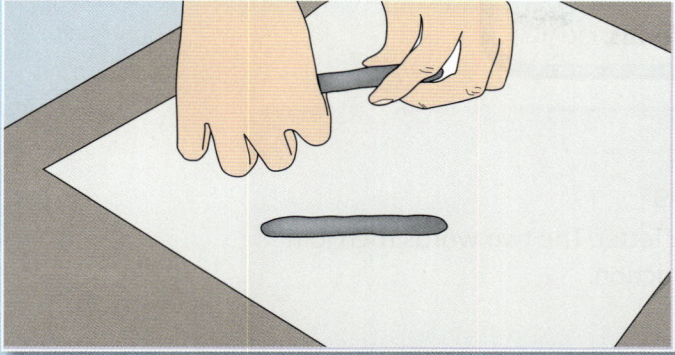

8 Curve the edges of the plate up, and place the support pieces around the edges underneath the paper.

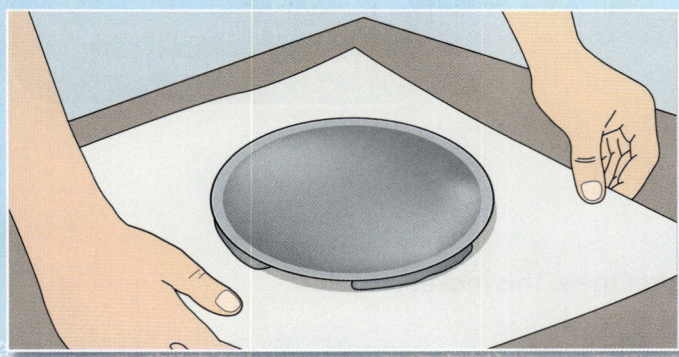

9 Use a piece of leather to smooth the edges of the plate.

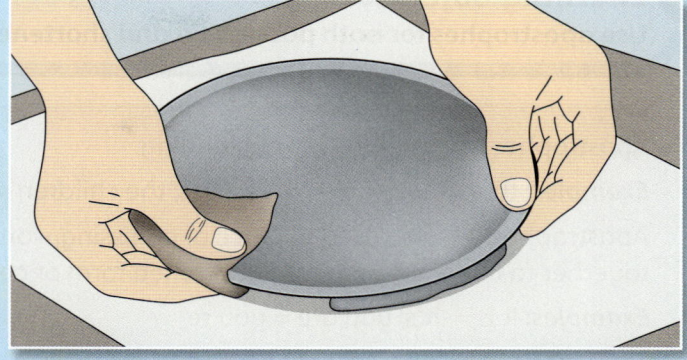

10 Let it dry and then take it to a kiln to be fired.

11 Paint your plate in a design of your choosing and fire it again.

Congratulations! You are a potter.

Comprehension

A

1 How many items (not including people) do you need to make and design the plate?

2 Why does the circular object need to be 'plate-sized'?

3 Where would the leftover clay come from?

B

Writer's language style

1 Which three different words tell the reader the order to do things in?

2 Instructions use 'bossy' (imperative) verbs such as 'cut' and 'chop' so that readers know what to do. Find six imperative verbs in the instructions.

3 What safety instructions could be added to the instructions?

C

What about you?

What traditional story from your country would you paint onto a plate?

Glossary

to fire when unglazed pottery or clay is put into a very hot oven and baked until it is hard

willow pattern a traditional blue pattern on chinaware telling a tale of long ago

Challenge

Give spoken instructions to a partner on how to do one of the following: play a game or sport; look after a pet. List any items needed. Use connectives and imperative verbs to make the actions clear.

Possessive apostrophes

 Learning objective
Use apostrophes for both possession and shortened forms.

Apostrophes are used to show belonging.

Examples: the man's house; girls' hats; the children's bags

Apostrophes are also used in place of a missing word or letter. The two words then join together to make one word – a shortened form or contraction.

Examples: it is = it's; you are = you're

A

Write out the following in the possessive apostrophe form.

Example: the dog belonging to the girl = the girl's dog

1   the tail belonging to the horse

2   the fields belonging to the farmer

3   the rice bag belonging to the lady

4   the supermarket belonging to the town

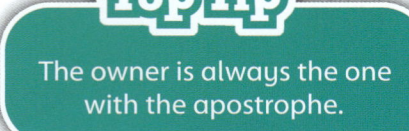
The owner is always the one with the apostrophe.

If the owner is plural, the apostrophe has to be placed after the **s**. This makes singular and plural owners look different for the reader.

Example: the boots belonging to the boy (singular) = the boy's boots

the boots belonging to the boys (plural) = the boys' boots

B

Write out the following in the plural possessive apostrophe form.

1   the dogs belonging to the girls

2   the tails belonging to the horses

3   the fields belonging to the farmers

4   the rice bags belonging to the ladies

C

Use each of the words below to write sentences using the possessive apostrophe.

children   men   women   sheep

Shortened form apostrophes

In *Tchang and the Pearl Dragon* there are some examples of apostrophes used where letters have been missed out of a word.

A

1 Write these contractions out in their full form. The first one has been done for you.

don't	do not
I'm	
I'll	
that's	
you're	
can't	
couldn't	

2 Which one of these reasons is correct? Apostrophes for shortened forms are used in texts because:

a it makes it easier to read.

b it reflects how people speak informally to one another.

c it varies things and makes it more interesting for the reader.

When *not* to use the apostrophe

With the plural non-possessive –s
Examples: tea's, cabbage's, flower's for sale ✗

With possessive pronouns
Examples: her's, their's, your's, it's ✗

shortened form **it is** = it's **use apostrophe**

possessive form **its** = **no apostrophe**

Half man, half spider

Learning objective
Begin to interpret imagery and techniques used by poets.

Word Cloud
cheats
tricks

Lillian Allen was born in Jamaica in 1951. She is a singer and songwriter as well as a poet, and today she lives in Canada.

Anancy the spiderman came from Africa. He is a trickster, hero and the chief character of many folk tales of the Caribbean.

Anancy

Anancy is a trickster of no small order
half a man and half a spider
Miss Muffet was sure glad
he hadn't sat beside her

5　He's unlike any of your friends
He's a whole lot smarter
He tricks and he outsmarts
He's a real fast talker

He's slow on his feet
10　a zip on his wit
When it comes to thinking quick
he's a wizard at tricks

He's never lost a game
'cause he cheats, double-crosses his friends
15　When he can't win fair
he's a spider again

Anancy is a trickster of no small order
half a man and half a spider
Miss Muffet was sure glad
20　he hadn't sat beside her

Lillian Allen

Glossary and idioms

double-crosses deceives people who trust the deceiver

of no small order extremely skilful and talented

outsmarts does cleverer things than other people

smarter cleverer

sure glad very pleased

trickster a person who plays tricks on others

zip on his wit very fast thinker

Comprehension

Give evidence from the poem to support your answers.

1 Sum up the 'story' of the poem in three sentences.

2 Why does the poet keep the first and last stanzas the same?

   a So they act like a chorus that the reader can remember easily

   b There is nothing new to say about Anancy.

   c Poems should always have the same beginning and ending.

3 Draw a box showing Anancy for each of the verses, so that, together, the boxes look like a comic strip.

   Examples:

   Verse 1: Anancy as half man, half spider

   Verse 2: Anancy with his mouth open as if talking

   Verse 3: Anancy as a wizard holding a wand

   Verse 4: Anancy hiding a card behind his back

   Verse 5: Miss Muffet with Anancy hiding quite far behind her

4 Choose one quotation from each verse and write this at the bottom of the box. It should match the drawing.

Poet's language technique

1 The poet has emphasized the 'trickster' part of Anancy. Find three words or phrases in the poem which show this.

2 The poet uses informal language as in real speech. Words are shortened using apostrophes. Find three different examples of contractions in the poem.

3 What effect does the informal language have on the reader?

What about you?

1 Would you be friends with Anancy? Explain your answer.

2 Tell your partner a folk story or fable that you know. Then swap and listen to his or her story.

135

Writing a traditional tale

 Learning objective
Write your own legend or fable using typical features of the genre.

Model writing

Look at the fable below. The story is mapped out so you can see how it moves along. Notice how the story is introduced, developed and taken to a climax. After that the problem is solved and we move to a conclusion.

Grandmother Spider: A Cherokee Tale

1 In the beginning there was only blackness, and nobody could see anything. People said: "What this world needs is light."

A The story begins with a traditional opener. The scene is set and the problem introduced.

2 Fox said some people on the other side of the world had plenty of light, but they were too greedy to share it. Possum said he would steal a little of it. "I have a bushy tail," he said. "I can hide the light inside all that fur."

B Characters are introduced. Dialogue makes it interesting and more realistic and moves the plot along when we tell the story.

3 Possum set out for the other side of the world. There he found the sun hanging in a tree and lighting everything up.

C The action moves forward and there is a happening from an imaginary world.

4 Possum sneaked over to the sun, picked out a tiny piece of light, and stuffed it into his tail. But the light was hot and burned all the fur off. Ever since, Possum's tail has been bald.

D The problem gets more complicated and there is a conclusion to the Possum's behaviour. Notice the strong verbs: 'sneaked' and 'stuffed'.

5 "I'll try," said Buzzard. I'll put it on my head." He flew off and, diving straight into the sun, seized the light with his claws and put it on his head. It burned his head feathers off. And ever since that time Buzzard's head has remained bald.

E There is repetition of the problem.

6 Grandmother Spider said, "Let me try!" First she made a clay pot. Next she spun a web reaching to the other side of the world. She was so small that nobody noticed her coming.

F We are moving towards a resolution to the problem. Connectors move the story along.

7 Quickly Grandmother Spider snatched up the sun, put it in the pot and scrambled back home along her web. Now her side of the world had light, and everyone rejoiced.

G Using lots of verbs close together gives the sense of speed and action.

8 Grandmother Spider brought not only the sun to the Cherokee, but fire as well. And, she taught the Cherokee people the art of pottery making.

H The problem is resolved and with an extra twist!

Guided writing

Think about these questions.

1 What is the main idea of your story?

2 Where does it take place? What is the setting?

3 Who are the main characters? What do they look like and how do they react to each other?

4 The plot: What is going to happen? Think of a problem or an obstacle that needs to be resolved or overcome. How will this happen?

5 What is the message of your story?

6 Language techniques: use imagery, metaphors and alliteration. Find examples in the story on pages 154–160 to help you.

Now write your story.

"My story is done. Let some go, let some come."
A saying from Africa

10 Fabulous future

What will happen if global warming continues?

Is this the spaceship of the future? You can see *SpaceShipTwo*, in the middle, suspended under the wing of the mothership, *WhiteKnightTwo*.

Space hotels and tourism of the future

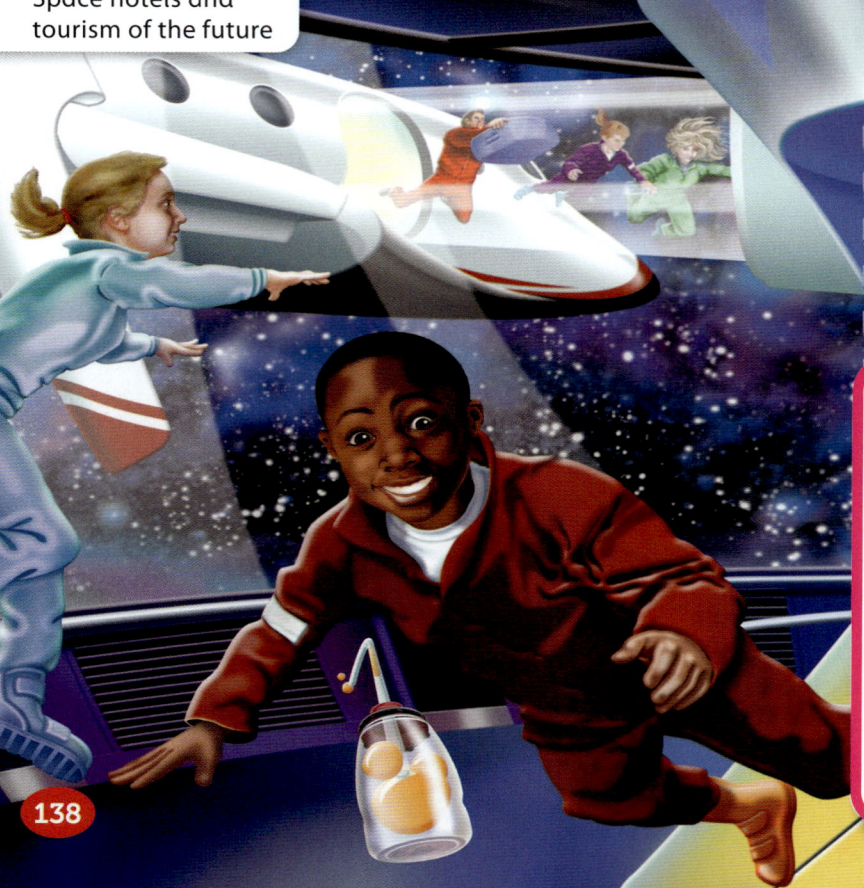

> "Children are the world's most valuable resource and its best hope for the future."
> John F. Kennedy,
> US President, 1961–1963

Let's Talk

Look at the pictures.

1 Describe what you can see in the first picture, top right.

2 What do you think has happened?

3 Where do you think people will go in a spacecraft like *SpaceShipTwo* in the future?

4 What would you show if you were asked to draw a picture of life in 50 years' time?

5 Why do you think children are the world's most valuable resource?

What do you predict?

Learning objective
Identify unfamiliar words, explore definitions and use new words in context.

Word Cloud

compass   imagine
experiments   motion sensor
future   nuclear reactor
GPS   predict
high-tech   robot
humanoid

It's fun to imagine what the future might be like. It is useful too. It makes you think. Will it be better, worse or just different? Films and games sometimes imagine a future where there has been a disaster. Global warming is one example.

New technologies, like those in the photos on this page, show us what the future might be like. The Internet may become more and more 'clever'. Space tourism could become common.

Science and technology might help us to prevent disasters and ensure a happy and exciting future.

What do you think will have happened by 2050 and what will we have invented?

Japanese students invented this Internet umbrella for fun. This umbrella has a camera, a motion sensor, a GPS and a compass in the handle. It will also show you a map in the top of the umbrella!

A

Match the words to the meanings. Use a dictionary to help you.

Example: 1e

1 humanoid robot
2 robotic arms
3 Nuclear reactor
4 high-tech
5 motion sensor
6 GPS (Global Positioning System)
7 compass

a artificial electronic arms
b satellite navigation
c new technology
d shows directions
e a machine which looks like a human
f used to make electricity
g knows when something is moving

B

Answer these questions in complete sentences.

1 What new inventions do you think we will have by 2050?
2 Do you think that the Internet umbrella is really useful, or just fun?
3 How do you think people will live in 2050?
4 How would you change the world if you could?

Asimo can serve drinks and dance. Robots work in places where it is unsafe for people to go, like nuclear reactors.

Future worlds: life on Venus

Learning objective
Comment on a writer's use of language and explain reasons for writer's choices.
Explore the features of different fiction genres.

Imagine living on a planet where rain falls continuously, except for one day every seven years – when the sun comes out for one hour. Such is life on the planet Venus where the children of settlers from Earth have grown up. The story takes place on that one day.

Word Cloud

bronze   squinted
civilization   wailed
savoured

All Summer in a Day

A thousand forests had been crushed under the rain and grown up a thousand times to be crushed again. And this was the way life was forever on the planet Venus, and this was the schoolroom of the children of the rocket men and women who had come to a raining
5 world to set up civilization and live out their lives.

"It's stopping, it's stopping!"…

The sun came out.

It was the colour of flaming bronze and it was very large. And the sky around it was a blazing blue tile colour. And the jungle burned
10 with sunlight as the children, released from their spell, rushed out, yelling, into the summertime.

"Now, don't go too far," called the teacher after them. "You've only one hour, you know. You wouldn't want to get caught out!"

But they were running and turning their faces up to the sky and
15 feeling the sun on their cheeks like a warm iron; they were taking off their jackets and letting the sun burn their arms.

"Oh, it's better than the sunlamps, isn't it?"

"Much, much better!"

They stopped running and stood in the great jungle that
20 covered Venus, that grew and never stopped growing, tumultuously, even as you watched it. It was a nest of octopuses, clustering up great arms of flesh-like weed, wavering, flowering in this brief spring. It was the colour of rubber and ash, this jungle from the many years without sun. It was the colour of stones and
25 white cheeses and ink.

The children lay out, laughing, on the jungle mattress, and heard it

sigh and squeak under them, resilient and alive. They ran among the trees, they slipped and fell, they pushed each other, they played hide-and-seek and tag but most of all they squinted at the sun until 30 tears ran down their faces, they put their hands up at that yellowness and that amazing blueness and they breathed of the fresh fresh air and listened and listened to the silence which suspended them in a blessed sea of no sound and no motion. They looked at everything and savoured everything. Then, wildly, like animals escaped from 35 their caves, they ran and ran in shouting circles. They ran for an hour and did not stop running.

And then —

In the midst of their running, one of the girls wailed.

Everyone stopped.

40 The girl, standing in the open, held out her hand.

"Oh, look, look," she said trembling.

They came slowly to look at her opened palm. In the centre of it, cupped and huge, was a single raindrop.

From *Science Fiction Stories* by Ray Bradbury

Comprehension

 A

Answer the questions using complete sentences.

1 Why had the children's parents come to Venus?
2 How did the children normally get their sunshine?
3 Why was the Venusian jungle the colour of rubber and ash?

 B

What do you think?

1 Why does the author describe the one hour of sunshine as 'summertime'?
2 Does the author succeed in describing the Venusian jungle? What words and phrases does he use to do this?
3 Why is science fiction so popular?

 C

What about you?

Can you imagine living in a place where it always rains? How would you manage?

Glossary

jungle a thick tangled forest, especially in tropical countries

palm the inner part of your hand, between your fingers and wrist

planet one of the bodies that move in an orbit round the sun. The main planets of the solar system are *Mercury, Venus, Earth, Mars, Jupiter, Saturn, Uranus* and *Neptune*

raindrop a single drop of rain

Personal pronouns

Learning objective
Use pronouns, making clear to what or whom they refer.

Personal pronouns indicate a person or a thing without naming it. So, rather than saying 'the boy' or 'the girl', we can use the pronouns 'he' and 'she'.

 A

The extract, 'All Summer in a Day', uses a lot of pronouns, so as to add to the mystery. Fill in the table below.

Pronoun	Number of times used
she	
they	
them	
you	
it	

 B

Pick out the personal pronouns in the sentences below and say which nouns they refer to.

Example: Fatima and Ahmed picked some apricots. They found them in a garden. (Fatima and Ahmed = they; apricots = them)

1 Tigger is a spaniel. He is only a puppy. The children are very fond of him.

2 When Mr and Mrs Smith sent Raphael a new bag he wrote to thank them for it.

3 Philippe had not seen Angelique's new car. He asked her to show it to him.

 C

In the following sentences replace the words underlined with personal pronouns.

1 Jasmin met <u>Javier and Alan</u>.

2 Mary met <u>Nasreen</u>.

3 <u>Wasim</u> met Mary.

4 <u>Leticia and I</u> met Angela.

5 <u>Sandeep and Jamelia</u> met Hilary.

6 Amelia and Belen met <u>Hilary and me</u>.

Possessive pronouns

Learning objective
Spell and make correct use of possessive pronouns.

Possessive pronouns are pronouns that show ownership.
Examples: **Yours** is over in the corner.
That chocolate is **mine**.

A

Pick out the pronouns in the sentences below. There are at least two in each sentence.

1 That book is mine, not yours.

2 Ours is way over there, so where are yours?

3 Everyone has different coloured shoes. Yours are black, hers are green.

4 Here is your car. Ours is over there. His is around the corner.

5 I found my key, but Mary couldn't find hers or his.

6 All the performances were good, but his and hers were the best.

B

Use the five pronouns you found in A in five sentences of your own.

C

As possessive pronouns focus on who owns things, they can appear more frequently in disagreements and arguments!

Two young children are arguing about who should have a book. Write their conversation!

A return ticket to space

Learning objective
Read and evaluate non-fiction texts for purpose, style, clarity and organization.

The golden ticket to outer space

Do you want to buy a ticket to become an astronaut? Five hundred people have already booked their trip. The first flights are due to take place in 2013 or 2014 from a spaceport in the United States. Passenger 500 will be film actor Ashton Kutcher who has just bought
5 his ticket. Tickets cost $200,000.

A new kind of spaceship

Richard Branson, a British airline owner and adventurer, has started a company called Virgin Galactic, which sounds like something from *Star Wars*. They have built the spacecraft like the one you can see in
10 the photo on page 138. The mothership, *WhiteKnightTwo*, has two compartments for crew, which look like two aeroplanes with a long wingspan in the middle. *SpaceShipTwo* is suspended from the middle of the wing.

How to become an astronaut

15 There will be two pilots and six passengers on *SpaceShipTwo*. *WhiteKnightTwo* will carry the spaceship up to 15.5 kilometres above the Earth, release it and go back to land. The spaceship's rocket will then propel it into space at up to 4,000 kilometres per hour. The passengers become astronauts at 100 kilometres above the Earth.
20 *SpaceShipTwo* will 'feather', or fold up, its wings. It will then fly higher to 110 kilometres and passengers will experience weightlessness for five minutes. They will be able to see the Earth's curve because they are so far away. Then the spaceship will re-enter the Earth's atmosphere. At 21.5 kilometres the wings will de-feather (open out)
25 so that it can glide down to the spaceport and land like a plane.

Word Cloud

adventurer   release
compartments   rocket
curve   suspended
glide   wingspan
propel

Glossary

astronaut a person who travels in a spacecraft

Galactic related to the galaxy

gravity the force that pulls everything towards the Earth

mothership the plane from which other spaceships are launched

spaceport an airport for spaceships

weightlessness to be free of the Earth's gravity so that you float about

The passenger cabin of *SpaceShipTwo*. If you are not strapped in you would float around. This is because you would be weightless as there is no gravity far from the Earth.

Comprehension

A

Answer in complete sentences.

1 How high does the mothership take *SpaceShipTwo* before it is launched?

2 How many people can fly on the spaceship?

3 When do the passengers become astronauts?

4 What makes passengers weightless?

B

What do you think?

1 Is it a good or a bad idea to take tourist trips into space?

2 In pairs, write down new headings for each paragraph of the extract.

C

What about you?

1 What do you think spacecraft might be used for in 30 to 50 years?

2 If there are people flying all round the world in spacecraft in the future, what will have to be done to keep them safe?

Let's Talk

Work in pairs

1 How does weightlessness and the lack of gravity make it difficult to live in a spaceship?

2 Make a list of the problems with a partner. One of you will report to the class.

The mothership carrying *SpaceShipTwo* into the air to be launched

Astronaut vocabulary

 Learning objective
Identify unfamiliar words, explore definitions and use new words in context.

A

Below are some words from the Word Cloud from the non-fiction extract, 'The golden ticket to outer space'. Can you put the letters for each word back in the right order?

saronautt   acespcrfta   lfghit   atmsoereph   trocke

B

All the words in A are connected to outer space.

Copy out the table and list six words which are connected to each of the bold headings. The first row has been done for you.

Health	Transport	School	Sport
hospital	car	class	tennis

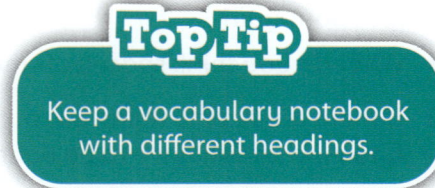
Keep a vocabulary notebook with different headings.

C

Write dictionary definitions of six words from one of the word lists you did for B so that the meanings of the words can be understood by young children.

Synonyms

Learning objective
Use a thesaurus to extend vocabulary and choice of words.

A thesaurus is a book of synonyms – words which have almost the same meaning.

Example: If you looked up 'thin', you would find words like slim, slender, slight, skinny and lean. There will also be the antonym (opposite) of thin: fat.

A

1 Unscramble the words below to find the six synonyms from a thesaurus for the word 'hot'.

bolingi   scrochnig   blistreing   siilngzz   arwm

itepd   wukelarm   sweeltirng   bruning

2 Which two words seem the least hot, and which two the hottest?

B

Here are some synonyms for the word 'cold'. Unscramble the letters to find them.

hillcy   ciy   frezeing   frsoty   niwtry   rozefn   biettr

C

These synonyms tell a reader whether it is hot or cold. However, your descriptions will be more effective if you show, rather than tell, it is hot or cold. *Example*: If you write, 'I felt cold'. You are telling the reader. If you write, 'I dug my fingers deeper into my pockets, desperately seeking warmth', you are showing the reader you are cold.

Write a sentence where you show that you are hot. Don't tell!

A poem for a blue planet

Learning objective

Comment on a writer's use of language and explain reasons for writers' choices.
Identify a point of view from which a story/poem is told.

Blue Planet's Blue

Boo hoo boo hoo,
Blue planet's blue.

Buckets of tears,
Tsunami is here.

5 Weep rant and wail,
Rhinos for sale.

Cry baby cry,
Forests will die.

Howl, yelp and screech,
10 Oil on the beach.

Watery eyes,
Sea levels rise.

Sob, sigh and whine,
Wildlife on the line.

15 Sighs and lamenting,
Climate is changing.

Sing a blue song,
Habitats gone.

Boo hoo hoo hoo,
20 Blue planet's real blue.

Hullabaloo,
It's all up to you!

Martin Kiszko

Word Cloud
habitats
lamenting
rant
wail

Comprehension

A

1 What pattern do the rhymes make in this poem?

2 What is the main message of the poem?

3 Read the last line. Now look at President Kennedy's
   words on page 138. What do they both mean?

4 How many problems does the poet mention?

5 Find at least 12 words which describe sounds.

Feel blue for our blue planet

B

Read the poem as a class. Then divide into two big groups. Read alternate verses.

C

1 In pairs, choose an animal or plant or part of the planet (such as ocean or rainforest) that you want to protect for the future.

2 Write two rhyming lines about the topic you have chosen. Use expressive 'sound' words in your first line as in the poem.

3 As a class, write down all the pairs of rhymes on the board until you have your own class Blue Planet poem.

4 Now read your lines out in pairs round the class.

Example: Shout yell and cry,

Or the tigers will die.

Glossary

blue to feel blue is to be sad

Blue Planet a name for the Earth (because it looks blue from space)

tsunami a big wave caused by an earthquake

Formal letters

Learning objective
Draft and write letters for real purposes.

The oil industry in the Delta region of Nigeria causes a lot of pollution. Villagers find it difficult to grow food. The pollution is also bad for their health.

The villagers want the oil company to stop polluting their land. The village chief wrote to the Managing Director of Southern Oil.

These villagers cannot grow vegetables any more or catch fish because of oil pollution.

Model writing
Answer the following questions about the format of a formal letter

How have the addresses been set out?

- What is the rule for using capital letters in addresses?
- Why has 'Pollution at Back Bay' been underlined?
- What is the purpose of the first paragraph?
- What is the purpose of the second paragraph?
- How should a formal letter be signed off?

Delta Council Building
PO Box 9500
Lagos

Mr M Danfodio
Southern Oil Company
Harbour Road, Back Bay   6 May, 2050

Dear Mr Danfodio,

Pollution at Back Bay

I am writing to inform you that the oil wells in Back Bay are still polluting our rivers and killing the fish. Oil is flooding the palm forests and the trees are dying. This is the third letter which we have sent. You have not replied.

The residents of Back Bay are going to take legal action and your company will be hearing from our lawyer shortly. They are also starting a campaign against your company.

I await your reply.

Yours sincerely,

James Otunde (Village Chief)

The future of the planet

Guided writing

1 Research an endangered animal (like the Indian tiger or the mountain gorilla).

2 Once you have done your research on an endangered animal, write a formal letter to a newspaper. Explain the threat to this animal and then suggest ideas for saving the animal from extinction. List the problems and suggested solutions clearly.

   ▶ In paragraph one, say what you are explaining about clearly. (Make a list first.)

   ▶ In paragraph two, say what you think should be done.

   ▶ In paragraph three, write a final sentence and a closing statement.

Your writing

Exchange your letter with a classmate and check that they have followed the correct format of a formal letter.

1 Write a formal letter to a newspaper explaining the problem. Say that it is important for the readers to know about this.

2 Design a poster to save the animal. Write a slogan – a phrase that people will remember.

The mountain gorilla is an endangered species. There are fewer than 800 left in the wild. There are seven billion of us!

151

Revise and check ③

Vocabulary

1 **Write out the sentences with the correct form of the adjective.**

a It was (beautiful) painting in the exhibition.

b Sara was (clever) at science than her brothers.

c The weekly newspaper is packed with the (late) stories.

d During the summer months it was (hot) and (wet) than in winter.

2 **Match and add another synonym of your own.**

say	chilly
eat	declare
walk	scorching
hot	gobble
cold	creep

3 **Match and write a sentence showing the meaning of each idiom.**

rags to	cake
piece of	riches
neck and	graces
airs and	neck

Punctuation

1 **Add commas to the sentences in the correct places.**

a A boy sat on the shore of a deep blue lake.

b "Oh what are we going to do?"

c Next morning Tchang's mother knew just what to do.

d She smiled at him but she did not reply.

e Since she was born she hasn't spoken a word.

f It was winter now and the snow lay thick upon the land.

Grammar

1 Write the text with all the verbs written out fully.

I'm sorry, I couldn't find the shop, but don't worry. There's a market close by and I'll buy more there. They weren't very expensive. You'll love them! They're bright yellow, like Adam's ones. We'll come over later; Harry's having lunch at his mum's house now.

2 Replace the underlined words with pronouns.

   a <u>Felix</u> saw his friends and stopped to pat the dog.

   b <u>The family</u> stayed in the cottage that belonged to Grandmother Betty.

   c "Don't touch the computer," <u>Aunt Ase</u> said. "It's grandma's."

3 Write the sentences with the correct word.

   a Where/wear are there/their boots?

   b We're not going there/they're today.

   c We're/where coming to/too!

   d There/their are too/two many people in that balloon!

Spelling

1 Write the sentences with the correct form of the verb.

Kirsty was (carry) a heavy parcel. Fin ran up and (grab) it from her. Kirsty (gasp). "I'm (try) to help," he told her. Then Fin (drop) the parcel! He looked up at Kirsty's face and saw that she was (cry). "Hey!" he said, "You're (worry) for nothing. I can fix anything!"

2 Choose the correct prefix and write the opposites of these words.

un– dis– in– il– ir– im–

   a legible   **d** believe

   b visible   **e** possible

   c comfortable   **f** regular

3 Write a sentence for each of the above words.

Tchang and the pearl dragon

A boy sat on the shore of a deep, blue lake in old China. He had been sitting there with his
5 fishing rod since sunrise but he hadn't caught a single fish. Wearily, he packed away his rod and trudged back to the little cottage where he lived.

Now it so happened that a great, green water dragon was passing by. It was on its way home to a far-off river. The dragon
10 had tiny wings and in its forehead was a huge pearl. The pearl flashed brightly in the sun – so brightly that the boy was dazzled and could not even see the dragon. He thought it was just the sun in his eyes.

The boy looked so unhappy that the dragon felt sorry for him.
15 He decided to follow the boy.

His mother was working in the garden, which was just a patch of dried-up dirt. She came running to greet him. "Well? What did you catch?"

He couldn't meet her eye. "Nothing, mother," he
20 replied miserably.

She slumped down on a log with her face in her hands. "Oh, what are we going to do? This land is dried up and dead. We don't have a thing to eat."

The boy was called Tchang. He and his mother slaved all day,
25 trying to scrape together enough to stay alive. But things were getting worse and worse. There were no longer any fish in the lake and very little grew in the barren soil.

The dragon overheard Tchang talking with his mother. Its heart went out to them. That night, when Tchang's mother was
30 sleeping, the dragon gently touched her brow with the tip of his magic wing.

Next morning, Tchang's mother knew just what to do. "You must go and visit the Great Wizard of the West," she told Tchang. "Ask him why we are so very, very poor when we work 35 so very, very hard."

So Tchang kissed his mother goodbye and set out for the West. He carried only a few scraps of bread wrapped up in a handkerchief.

For forty-nine days Tchang trudged across deserts and over 40 mountains until he came to a dark forest. His bread had run out long ago and he was so tired and hungry, he could hardly walk.

Eventually, he reached a tiny house. In the yard, a lovely young girl was drawing water from a well. "Hello, there!" Tchang called. She smiled at him, but she did not reply.

45 An old lady appeared at the door of the house. "I see you've met my granddaughter, Ai-li," she called. "Please don't mind that she didn't greet you. Since the day she was born, she hasn't spoken a word. It makes me very sad."

Then she looked closely at Tchang. "You look worn out! 50 Come inside and have a bite to eat."

That evening Tchang sat by the fire. He told the pair that he was on his way to ask the Great Wizard of the West a question.

"Good for you!" cried the old woman. "While you're there, could you ask him why Ai-li can't talk?"

55 The next day, Tchang set off once again towards the West.

Another forty-nine days passed. The food the old lady gave him soon ran out. Finally, he saw a little hut in the middle of an orchard that was scorched brown by the sun. The land looked so dry and poor, it reminded him of home. An old man appeared

60 in the doorway of the hut. "Boy!" he called. "You look worn out! Come inside and rest."

Later, Tchang told the old man where he was going. "You're a good boy to undertake such a difficult journey," said the old man. "By the way, when you see the Wizard, would you mind
65 asking him why my lemon tree won't bear fruit?"

Tchang agreed, of course.

Next morning, he rose early and set off once more for the West. After yet another forty-nine days he came to a river, fast and deep and wide. His heart sank. There was no way he could
70 cross it.

Suddenly, a great green dragon rose from the water. Even to Tchang, who had never met a dragon before, its tiny wings seemed too small for its body. Set in its forehead was a gorgeous pearl.
75 Tchang was about to run away, but the dragon called to him. "Don't be frightened! I'm quite harmless. Tell me why you want to cross my river."

Tchang explained that he needed to ask the Great Wizard of the West some important questions.

80 When the Pearl Dragon heard the questions, it smiled. "You're a good lad, Tchang," it said. "Hop on my back and I'll have you across in a jiffy."

On the far side of the river, Tchang thanked the dragon.

"Think nothing of it!" the dragon replied cheerfully. "That's
85 what I'm here for. Oh, by the way. While you're there, could you please ask the Wizard why I can't fly? Every dragon in China can fly – except me."

Naturally, Tchang said yes. He set off again towards the West with the four questions going around and around in his head.

90 Forty-nine days later, he came to the golden palace of the Great Wizard of the West. The palace was carved out of a mountain. It took Tchang a whole day to climb the million steps up to the huge door. When he pulled on the bell rope, the
95 mountain shook. Flocks of eagles rose squawking into the air from a thousand golden towers.

The great doors of the palace swung open. Tchang found himself in a mighty hall. It was so high he couldn't see the ceiling for clouds. On a throne at the end of the hall sat the Great
100 Wizard. He glared down at Tchang. "Well?" he bellowed. "What do you want, boy?"

Tchang tried to stop shaking. "I … I have four questions to ask you, sir!"

"HAH!" shouted the Wizard. "Then you may as well go
105 home right now! I will only answer THREE questions. If you
ask me four, I won't answer any of them. So there!"

Tchang thought his legs would fold underneath him. What
could he do? There was his poor mother's question, then the
old woman's question, then the old man's question, and then
110 the Pearl Dragon's question. For his own sake, as well as his
mother's, he desperately wanted to know the answer to the first
question – but he also knew he couldn't let his friends down. So
he answered sadly, "Then I will only ask you three."

When Tchang had asked his questions a thunderstorm began
120 to rage high up in the hall. The Wizard hurled three scrolls
down to Tchang. "Here are your answers, boy. Now go home!"

Tchang fled from the palace. He leaped down the million
stone steps, five at a time.

When he reached the river, the Pearl Dragon was waiting for
125 him. "Well?" it said. "What did the Wizard say?"

Tchang opened the scroll marked 'Dragon'. "He says, if you
do something really kind and generous, you'll be able to fly like
other dragons."

"Hmm," said the Dragon. "Well, hop aboard and I'll take you
130 across the river."

At the other side, it reached up and prised the great pearl
from its forehead. "This is the only precious thing I possess,"
it said to Tchang. "I'd like you to take it, but
when you get home, you must throw it into
135 the lake."

As the dragon handed the pearl to
Tchang, its wings grew and grew until
it rose slowly into the air. "Look!"
it shouted joyfully, "I can fly!"

140 It was winter, now, and snow lay
thick upon the land. Tchang struggled
on towards the East until he
reached the old man's hut.

The old man was delighted to see him. "So? What did the Wizard say?"

Tchang opened the scroll marked 'Old Man'. "He says you must look beneath the lemon tree."

Together they dug at the frozen earth around the tree until they came upon nine golden jars. Water poured from them, as clear as crystal. As it sank into the ground, all the trees in the orchard burst into flower.

The old man was so grateful he gave Tchang one of the golden jars.

Tchang travelled on until he reached the little house in the forest. Ai-li was away tending the sheep. The old woman said, "So why can't Ai-li speak?"

Tchang opened the scroll marked 'Old Woman'. He replied, "She will speak when she loves someone with all her heart."

Then the door opened and there stood Ai-li. "Tchang!" she cried.

The old woman was overjoyed. She told Tchang, "You should marry my granddaughter. She will make you a wonderful wife."

So Tchang and Ai-li were married.

Then they set off again towards the East. Eventually, they reached Tchang's home. His mother didn't see them coming –
170 she had cried for so long, she had gone blind.

Tchang's heart was heavy. How would he tell her that he hadn't even asked the Wizard her question? Then he remembered the pearl. As he took it from his pocket, the light from the pearl shone into his mother's eyes and
175 suddenly she could see again.

Remembering what the dragon had told him, Tchang ran to the lake. He threw the pearl into its deep blue waters. The lake seemed to shudder and heave. Then Tchang saw that it was teeming with fine, fat fish that jumped right out of the water
180 onto the shore.

Tchang unpacked the golden jar. The crystal clear water poured out onto the garden and a forest of flowers sprang from the earth.

Their troubles were finally over. Tchang lived with his mother
185 and Ai-li and their children for many long and happy years. And every day, the Pearl Dragon would soar high overhead and smile down upon them.

From *Dragon Tales* by Andy Blackford